PICKING UP
THE PIECES

Stephanie A.N. Levin

PICKING UP
THE PIECES

Finding My Way as a Visually Impaired Woman in Higher Education

The Disability Studies Collection

Collection Editors

Damian Mellifont
&
Jennifer Smith-Merry

LPp

To my Mom, Dad, Granny, Cecil, and Mason (the boys): Thank you for always believing in me even when I did not believe in myself.

First published in 2025 by Lived Places Publishing
All rights reserved. No part of this publication may be reproduced, stored in a retrieval system, or transmitted in any form or by any means, electronic, mechanical, photocopying, recording or otherwise, without prior permission in writing from the publisher.

No part of this book may be used or reproduced in any manner for the purpose of training artificial intelligence technologies or systems. In accordance with Article 4(3) of the Digital Single Market Directive 2019/790, Lived Places Publishing expressly reserves this work from the text and data mining exception.

The author and editors have made every effort to ensure the accuracy of information contained in this publication, but assume no responsibility for any errors, inaccuracies, inconsistencies, and omissions. Likewise, every effort has been made to contact copyright holders. If any copyright material has been reproduced unwittingly and without permission the Publisher will gladly receive information enabling them to rectify any error or omission in subsequent editions.

Copyright © 2025 Lived Places Publishing

British Library Cataloguing in Publication Data
A CIP record for this book is available from the British Library

ISBN: 9781916985902 (pbk)
ISBN: 9781916985926 (ePDF)
ISBN: 9781916985919 (ePUB)

The right of Stephanie A.N. Levin to be identified as the Author of this work has been asserted by them in accordance with the Copyright, Design and Patents Act 1988.

Cover design by Fiachra McCarthy
Book design by Rachel Trolove of Twin Trail Design
Typeset by Newgen Publishing UK

Lived Places Publishing
P.O. Box 1845
47 Echo Avenue
Miller Place, NY 11764

www.livedplacespublishing.com

Abstract

Author Stephanie Levin provides an overview of disability history within higher education settings and explains the impact of poor care on disabled students. Stephanie was only 20 years old when she experienced retinal detachment. At 22, Stephanie experienced a second retinal detachment in the same eye which resulted in vision loss. With her newfound identity as a visually impaired woman, Stephanie struggled with her mental health and wellbeing. She refused university accommodations for fear of stigmatization, yet she found that individuals close to her viewed her differently. Through themes of identity and trauma, this book is ideal for carers, teachers, scholar-practitioners, disabled students, and students of Disability Studies and Education.

Keywords

Disability; university; college; barriers to learning; PTSD; eye surgery; retinal detachment; mental health; identity; lived experience

Contents

Content warning

This book contains explicit references to, and descriptions of, situations which may cause distress. This includes references to and descriptions of:

- Suicidal ideation
- Post-traumatic stress disorder, depression, and anxiety
- Ableism and stigmatization

Every effort has been made to provide more specific content warnings before relevant chapters, but please be aware that references to potentially distressing topics occur **frequently throughout** the book.

Introduction

Hello everyone! Welcome to my book! It is an honor to tell you my story and to educate you on the realm of disability within higher education. At this point, I would like to formally introduce myself. My name is Stephanie, and I am visually impaired. How I became visually impaired is a story in and of itself. On June 11, 1992, unknown to my parents, I was born with a condition called lattice degeneration. Simply put, lattice degeneration occurs when one's peripheral retina is irregularly thin (The American Society of Retina Specialists, 2024a).

This condition causes the perimeter of one's retina to look like a lattice fence, and it is commonly found in people who are myopic or severely nearsighted. Approximately ten percent of individuals are affected by lattice degeneration (Porter and Gregori, 2023). Unfortunately, lattice degeneration can result in retinal detachment which is when the retina disconnects from the back eye cavity (The American Society of Retina Specialists, 2024b). This is the moment where my story begins.

The beginning of a new direction

What I am about to tell you is not a pretty story, but you must know the entire truth. I would like to take you back to 2012. Prior to my experiences, I was just like any typical college student. I was 20 years old, and I was currently enrolled at a state university in South Jersey. I was in the process of completing my bachelor of science in business management with a minor in theater studies. I was fearless, and I felt that I was ready to make my mark on the world. I did not know what that mark would be, but I was determined to make some sort of impact on the society. However, my life path took a different turn.

I remember the day that everything changed. It was August 9, 2012. A day or two prior, I had told my mom that I had been seeing a black curtain in the field of my vision within my right eye. My primary eye doctor was not available to see me, so I was seen by another eye doctor within the existing practice. As my mom and I were sitting in the waiting area, my mom leaned over to me and said, "After this appointment, you will go home and rest your eyes." I nodded in agreement, and a few minutes later, my name was called. The eye doctor came in, examined my dilated eyes. She informed my mom and me that I had a slightly detached retina. My mom had asked the eye doctor if anything needed to be done to correct this problem. I sat frozen in my seat as she said the following: "Stephanie will need immediate surgery. Without surgery, your daughter will lose her vision." I looked at my mom in disbelief, and I started to cry. In fact, we both cried as my eye doctor informed us that I needed to see a retina specialist that evening. My mom, with shaking hands, called my dad and told him the news. My dad, who was in shock, said to my mom, "How could you let this happen to my daughter?" Now I know how this statement might sound to some of you. Please understand that my dad was in shock. He was just delivered some extremely difficult news that is hard to process at face value. He did not know what retinal detachment was nor had he ever heard of this condition. He was scared, and he did not know what the future was to hold.

That evening, my mom and I drove to the retina specialist. To say that I was hysterical is an understatement of the century. As I sat in the car and cried, I wondered how I would ever get through this. To make matters worse, I was still fully dilated from my eye doctor appointment. At the time, I wore contacts in both eyes. I did not put my contacts back in for fear that the contact in my right eye would make the detachment worse. Of course, I did not have my glasses with me. As a result, I could not see anything. I walked into the retina specialist's office, and everything looked blurry to me. All of these new faces were staring back at me, and I could not see their features. That alone was a terrifying experience. As I lay on the chair while my retina specialist examined my eyes, I squirmed under the bright lights and the discomfort. I felt so vulnerable and scared. After the examination, my retina specialist told me that I would need a scleral buckle implant inserted in my right eye. A scleral buckle is a piece of rubber, semi-firm, plastic, or sponge that is made out of silicone. The purpose of this buckle is to flatten the retina or to close any breaks. An ophthalmologist will sew this piece of material to the outside area of the eye, and it stays in one's eye on a permanent basis (HealthLink BC, n.d.). It was also decided that my left eye was to be lasered so that I would not experience a retinal detachment in that eye. Upon hearing this news, my anxiety significantly increased, but I knew that in order to save my vision, I had to undergo this surgery.

A few minutes later, we were directed to another room. The retina specialist's liaison walked my family and me through the surgery and the recovery time. In a shaky voice, my mom said to the liaison, "I am so scared. Is my daughter going to be alright? She is my only child, and she is my baby." Hearing my mom say that statement broke my heart. To this very day, I cannot help but remember those words and tear up. That night, as I prepared for my surgery, I prayed that I would be okay. I prayed for some inner strength that I subconsciously knew that I would need to draw from.

Surgery number one

On August 10, 2012, I underwent my first retinal detachment surgery at Wills Eye Hospital in Philadelphia, Pennsylvania. The day after my eye surgery, I had to return to Wills Eye for my post-op appointment. I am not exaggerating when I tell you that the pain from the scleral buckle was excruciating. My dad drove my mom and me to the hospital. My mom was sitting in the back with me, and I was lying down on the seats. Every bump that my dad drove over resulted in me screaming from the pain and the anger that had enveloped me. I was on multiple eye drops to prevent inflammation and infection. My eye was weeping lymphatic fluid, and the gauze which acted as a cushion between the plastic eye covering and my eye needed to be changed every few hours. My mom had to administer the eye drops because I could not do anything for myself. It was as if I had regressed into childhood. I learned later after my first surgery that my mom would help me with my eye drops and go into the downstairs bathroom and cry so that I would not see how upset she was over this ordeal. That was another piece of information that completely devastated me.

A few weeks later, after I had initially recovered from my surgery, my retinal specialist provided me with clearance to return to school. I remember being so excited because back then, I had this fear that all of my friends and acquaintances were moving forward in their college careers, and I was stuck in time. I was determined to show others that I was okay. I convinced myself that this situation was just a blip in the radar system. Why I cared so much about what others thought about me at the time I will never know. All I know is that I was young, impressionable, and more vulnerable than I had originally thought. I returned to school grateful that I had overcome this obstacle, and I thought that the worst was behind me. How wrong I was to assume such a thing.

Surgery number two

The second surgery really caught me by surprise. I did not think that I would find myself back in that place. However, life is funny that way. In December 2014, a little over a week before Christmas, something did not feel or look right in my right eye's field of vision. My right eye had some sensitivity to light, and it felt uncharacteristically heavy. So, I informed my mom that something was wrong, and we immediately made an appointment to see my eye doctor. Once again, my primary eye doctor was not available to see me that day; however, another eye doctor was on call. Ironically, it was the same eye doctor who found my first retinal detachment. Sadly, this same eye doctor informed my mom and me that I had a retinal tear. I sat in that chair in disbelief. I thought to myself, "How could this happen again? Why was this happening to me? Am I defective?" Also, I was extremely angry.

I was not the most pleasant person to be around that day, and even now, I regret my behavior. I just could not understand why this was happening to me. My retina specialist had explained to me that scar tissue had built up around my scleral buckle, and it had pulled on the implant which resulted in a tear.

On that cold December day in 2014, I underwent laser surgery to repair my retinal tear. As the laser evoked a stinging, burning sensation in my eye, I could hear Don McLean's (1971) song *American Pie* playing on the radio. My retina specialist worked diligently as the lyrics of this beautiful song blared on the speaker. It really is amazing how one notices all of the little details in times of trauma. All of the little nuances one would miss during periods of monotony are suddenly revealed. I wish that I could tell you that this was the end of my story, but unfortunately, it is not so. The laser that was meant to fix the tear did not hold. On December 24, 2014, while other families were watching *It's a Wonderful Life* with Jimmy Stewart and Donna Reed, I was experiencing my second retinal detachment. I felt a painful, ripping sensation in my right eye, and I rushed to the bathroom to do the eye check that my retina specialist had instructed me to do to see if there were any changes in my field of vision. As soon as I looked in the mirror in the bathroom, I knew that there was a problem. The tear had morphed into the characteristic black curtain that I had seen two years ago. I spent a sleepless night hoping that I was wrong. I still remember waking up the next morning full of fear and anguish. That Christmas was the worst Christmas that I had ever experienced. I spent my holiday checking my eye and trying to conceal the fact that there was a problem. In addition to my eye issues, my granny's colon cancer had returned, and we knew that this would be our last Christmas with her. Eventually, I told my parents that something was terribly wrong. The next day, on December 26, 2014, I had an appointment with the retina specialist on call, and he had informed me that my retina was detached, and this time, the detachment was going into my macula, or the central area of my vision (Cleveland Clinic, 2022b). I was so angry about my predicament that I initially refused surgery, but my mom was not having any of it. As I look back, I realize how incredibly ridiculous it was to initially refuse surgery. That surgery afforded me so many opportunities, and it provided me with a great quality of life. I was just so very scared.

My parents had to pay out of pocket for my second surgery because there was no one available to authorize the surgery within the insurance company. We unsuccessfully tried to appeal against this payment; however, our appeal was denied. That same day, I underwent a vitrectomy which is a procedure that involves the removal of the vitreous gel in the eye. This gel is replaced with another substance such as a gas bubble, saline, or silicone oil (Johns Hopkins Medicine, 2024). In my case, a gas bubble was used to keep the retina in place. For five days, I needed to lay on my left side so that the gas bubble would allow the retina to be locked in place. To this day, I cannot lie on the left side because it brings back so many unpleasant memories. Gas bubbles usually take a few months to completely dissipate. For me, it was a period of four months. Because of my surgery, I needed to take a semester off from school, and I was able to resume my studies in summer 2015. During my recovery time, my granny succumbed to cancer, and she left us on February 24, 2015. My gramps, who was my dad's father, passed away 16 hours prior to my granny on

February 23, 2015. I remember trying so hard to keep it together. I wanted to show everyone that I was alright and that I was the same Stephanie as before. However, the truth is I was not the same. I was psychologically traumatized, I suffered from vision loss, and I had so many unresolved feelings about my experiences. People treated me differently, and my competence was questioned. I did not know what to do, and I did not know how to put the pieces back together. The stigma and discrimination that I was experiencing were real, and I felt so alone.

Present day

My story continued to impact my life in more ways than one. It took me years to come to terms with what had happened to me. I am a firm believer that everything happens for a reason, and I knew in my heart that I was meant to help others who were going through similar experiences as my own. Fast forward a few years later, it was always a dream of mine to obtain my doctorate in Educational Leadership. At the age of 30, I was accepted into Rowan University's Ed.D. program. During orientation, as we were all sitting in our seats, the professor asked us this question: "What is a problem of practice within your sphere of influence?" As I sat there thinking about what my problem of practice might be, a light bulb went off in my head. It was at that moment that I decided to focus on college students who have visual impairments and who, like me, have experienced mental health, stigma, discrimination, and identity crises surrounding their disability.

Since the beginning of this program, I have made it my mission to raise awareness regarding the numerous struggles that we, as a community, have endured. This is a timely problem that needs our attention. It is true that the disability population often goes unnoticed (Shallish, 2015). I often ask why that is. Why do higher education administrators and society as a whole continue to ignore the oppression and the struggles that this community experiences? I believe that this ever-pressing issue needs to change now, which is why I have decided to write this book. It is necessary for me to add to the existing disability rhetoric and literature, and to provide you with a real-life narrative that is interwoven with important research on the disability population.

What this book is about

My book seeks to educate you about my disability of being visually impaired as well as about disability more broadly within higher education. Each chapter has a specific theme that it will focus on, and I will intertwine my own personal experience navigating higher education as a visually impaired woman. In Chapter 1, I will provide you with an overview of disability history within the realm of higher education. Chapter 2 will focus on the present-day terrain of disability at the college and university levels. In Chapter 3, I will shift gears, and I will define what it means to be visually impaired. Additionally, I want to introduce you to the different types of visual impairments as I believe that we need to have a general understanding of them. Chapter 4 will focus on disability stigma and ableism that are often experienced by students with disabilities in higher education. In addition, I will provide you with my own personal experiences of how I endured stigma and ableism as an undergraduate and graduate student. Chapter 5 will cover the barriers that visually impaired higher education students experience on their college and university campuses. Some of these barriers include issues pertaining to admissions, accommodations, technology, and socialization. A general definition of the term *barrier* will be provided, and I will highlight what the word *barrier* means within the context of disability. I will also discuss the medical and social models of disability.

Chapter 6, and I am sorry to say this, is where it gets a little dark. Within this chapter, I am going to provide you with definitions of post-traumatic stress disorder, anxiety, and depression. In addition, I will discuss how visually impaired higher education students are affected by these psychological disorders. Now I am going to be honest with you. I, too, experienced all three of these disorders due to the trauma from my retinal surgeries. Only a few people truly know the extent of the psychological pain that I had experienced from these ordeals. What I am going to reveal about my experiences will come as a shock to many people, but I feel that telling you about my experiences is necessary, and I hope others who are in similar predicaments to mine understand that they are not alone.

Chapter 7 will discuss how I had to reconstruct my identity as a visually impaired woman, and I will emphasize how important it is to have a strong support system around you when dealing with life-altering events such as this. Chapter 8 will highlight how advocacy and empathy are needed to address disability within higher education. Ways that all-inclusiveness can be promoted for students with disabilities at the higher education level will also be discussed. I will conclude with a summary of the key messages of this book.

At the end of this book, I will provide you with five interesting discussion questions and assignments that will help you to think about the material presented within this book. Also, I feel it is important that I share with you a few specific resources that may be of help to you. While I was going through my own experiences with visual impairment, I felt isolated and misunderstood. I do not want anyone to feel the same way that I had felt during my experiences. So, I would like to present you with the names and contact information for a few advocacy groups that are specifically for the blind and visually impaired. Additionally, I will include important information pertaining to the Suicide and Crisis Lifeline and the National Domestic Violence Hotline and website. Finally, I will provide you with a retinal detachment support group page that can be found on Facebook. I want you to understand that you do not have to endure your hardships alone. If you are struggling in any way, shape, or form, please know that there is help and that there are so many people who care for you. You bring so much light and love to this world, and I do not want you to ever forget that.

I want to thank you for getting acquainted with my story. Your reading this introduction means so much to me. Now it is time to move forward and to begin the journey of truly understanding visual impairments within the context of higher education. In the words of Dan Quayle, who was the 44th United States vice president, "We will move forward, we will move upward, and yes, we will move onward" (Dowd, 1996).

Learning objectives

This book is written to assist readers to:

- Describe disability history and the current context of disability within higher education today.
- Recognize the different forms of visual impairment.
- Recognize the psychological challenges of the visually impaired higher education student.
- Recall the current barriers and stigma of the visually impaired within the context of higher education.
- Learn how to become an advocate of the visually impaired and for the disabled population as a whole.

1
Disability history in higher education: The good, the bad, and the ugly

Sir Walter Scott, a Scottish author and poet, is credited with a well-known phrase from his poem titled *Marmion*. Within his ode, this infamous poet provides us with the following verse: "Oh what a tangled web we weave" (Wise, 2021, p. S24). As I began preparing to write this chapter, this very phrase came to mind. The history of disability within the context of higher education is quite an intricate story. I could probably devote an entire course book explaining to you the many nuances of the disability time-line; however, that is not what this book is about. Instead, I want to provide you with an overview of disability history, and to help you to understand the many highlights that comprise this realm within higher education. I hope that you find this first chapter insightful, and that you learn many important points regarding disability. Now, everyone, before I start, I must ask you these questions: Are you sitting in a comfortable position? Did you grab a snack? If so, let us begin!

Thomas Hopkins Gallaudet: Pioneer for the deaf

Our timeline begins with a man named Thomas Hopkins Gallaudet Gallaudet was born in 1787 in Philadelphia, Pennsylvania. After completing his undergraduate and graduate studies at Yale College, he attempted to work at a law practice in Hartford, Connecticut. Unfortunately, he had to quit his job because he was sickly. As a result of this issue, Gallaudet earned his degree in theology from a school in Massachusetts known as the Andover Theological Seminary. Due to his ongoing health issues, Gallaudet could not take on a roll as a permanent pastor. Instead, he often traveled to convey his ministry, and he visited towns in the Northeast. In addition to his ministry, he taught US history and theology to children who did not have teachers (Gifford, 2021).

During 1815–1816, while in Hartford, Connecticut, Gallaudet met Alice Cogswell. Cogswell was nine years old, and she became deaf due to a disease known as spotted fever (Gallaudet, 1888). Gallaudet did something that was considered extremely progressive for the nineteenth century. To be honest, the man was way beyond his time. Gallaudet began teaching Cogswell. He taught her how to write words using a stick in the dirt! He also furthered her knowledge of words by pointing at different objects (Gifford, 2021).

Gallaudet, pictured below in figure 1 (Wright, 1851), was also interested in specific experiments that were taking place in Europe. These experiments pertained to the creation of signals and signs which would allow communication among the mute and the deaf! At the insistence of Cogswell, Gallaudet traveled to Europe, and he began studying these schools that were specifically for the deaf. While on his trip, Gallaudet met Abbott Roch-Ambroise Cucurron Sicard. Sicard, pictured in figure 2 (abbé R.A.L. 1742–1842), was a Catholic Priest from France, and he served as the leader for the Royal Institution for Deaf-Mutes. This institution was located in Paris, France, and Gallaudet was invited to study with the faculty of this institution (Gifford, 2021).

Figure 1. Posthumous oil painting of Thomas Hopkins Gallaudet (Wright, 1851)

Figure 2. Sicard (abbé R.A.L. 1742–1842)

One of the faculty members who was tutoring Gallaudet was Father Laurent Clerc. At the time, Father Clerc, who was deaf, was in the process of creating a premature sign language manual. Gallaudet and Father Clerc returned to America, and they began to acquire funding for a school for the deaf. In 1817, the Connecticut Asylum for the Education and Instruction of Deaf and Dumb Persons was opened in Bennett's City Hotel. However, Gallaudet was not happy about the school's location or name. Luckily, the United States Congress provided a grant for the school which allowed the institution to relocate to a piece of land in West Hartford, Connecticut. In addition, the school's name was changed to the American School for the Deaf in 1821 (Gifford, 2021).

Edward Miner Gallaudet: Following in his father's footsteps

It was in the middle of the nineteenth century when the number of schools for the deaf substantially increased throughout the United States. This increase in deaf institutions brought forth a wave of activists who pushed for the rights of deaf high school students to attend higher education establishments (de Lorenzo, 2009, cited in Evans et al., 2017). In the year 1864, significant changes occurred. The 16th President of the United States, Abraham Lincoln, endorsed a legislation which allowed a college department to be created within "the Columbia Institution for the Deaf and Dumb" (Madaus, 2011, p. 5). This department was named "the National Deaf-Mute College" (Evans et al., 2017, p. 20). Edward Miner Gallaudet, Thomas Gallaudet's son, was credited for awarding college degrees to those who attended this institution. The first student was admitted to the college during the autumn of 1864. In 1866, this enrollment increased to 25 students. Two of these students were women and all 25 pupils hailed from Washington, D.C. as well as 13 other states (Gallaudet, 1983, cited in Madaus, 2011).

Edward Gallaudet had what I would like to call a full-circle moment. In the year 1894, the National Deaf-Mute College was renamed Gallaudet College after Thomas Hopkins Gallaudet. Thomas H. Gallaudet was the father of Edward M. Gallaudet (de Lorenzo, 2009, cited in Evans et al., 2017). In 1962, a graduate curriculum was created. There was a specific purpose for this program that was provided to deaf students. Fundamentally speaking, this program paved the way for deaf pupils to obtain employment and acquire knowledge (de Lorenzo, 2009; Madaus, 2000; 2011, cited in Evans et al., 2017). Initially, students who were blind were accepted to Gallaudet College; however, one year later, these pupils were relocated to the Maryland Institute in Baltimore (Griffin et al., 2007, cited in Evans et al., 2017).

The Great War (1914–1918)

Let us move forward to the early twentieth century. Soldiers who have served their country during times of war have exhibited increased health risks, psychological problems, and significant challenges associated with personally and educationally adjusting to their surroundings. From an educational adjustment standpoint, veterans have faced challenges establishing on-campus connections with faculty and students (Barry, Whiteman, and Wadsworth, 2014). The Great War, also known as the First World War, established that disability was quite an extensive topic; however, it was a topic that was questioned by society on a regular basis. Individuals with disabilities were described as those who were functionally impaired (Hickel, 2001; Longmore, 2003; Pelka, 2012, cited in Evans et al., 2017).

The Veterans Vocational Rehabilitation Act

Let us start with some good news surrounding the topic of disability within higher education. During the year 1918, the Veterans Vocational Rehabilitation Act was passed by the federal government! This Act was significant because it assisted disabled veterans with their education (Chatterjee and Mirta, 1998, cited in Madaus, 2011). In addition, the ratification of this law allowed veterans to study agriculture, trade, and industry. Veterans who had previous higher education experience were able to obtain specialized training (Gelber, 2005, cited in Madaus, 2011).

Ohio Mechanics Institute

Another excellent piece of news regarding disability history pertains to the Ohio Mechanics Institute! Located in Cincinnati, Ohio, this institution admitted more than 400 First World War disabled veterans (Madaus, 2011, cited in Evans et al., 2017). These pupils were also forward-thinking individuals because they created a group known as the Disabled American Veterans. The mission of this organization is to inspire veterans to live quality lives on the basis of dignity and respect (Disabled American Veterans, 2024). These students truly set the foundation for self-advocation which is important within the world of disabilities. We will discuss self-advocation in a later chapter.

The Veterans Bureau

Now, this is where disability history can get quite unpleasant. In 1921, the Veterans Bureau was enacted. Colonel Charles R. Forbes, pictured in Figure 4 (Library of Congress, 1909), served as the 1st United States Veterans Bureau director. Forbes was sworn into this position on August 9, 1921 (Stevens, 2017). The reason for establishing a bureau such as this was to verify that benefits were reasonably granted to those who were included within the disabled community. Unfortunately, the Veterans Bureau exercised total control over the pensions that were granted to veterans with disabilities. In addition, by viewing disabled veterans, pictured below in Figure 3 (National Museum of Health and Medicine, 1919, as functionally impaired, procedures and policies that promoted stigmatism and segregation were enacted. Another unfortunate piece of news is that society was concerned that veterans with disabilities were going to become a public burden (Ward, 2009, cited in Evans et al., 2017). This statement saddens me to the core. To think that a soldier goes off to war, serves their country, and then returns home physically and mentally traumatized is bad enough. However, to feel like they are nothing but an inconvenience to the public upon their return is truly terrible.

Figure 3. Disabled WWI veteran at Walter Reed General Hospital (Otis Historical Archives, National Museum of Health and Medicine, circa 1919)

Figure 4. Col. Charles R. Forbes, Director, US Veterans' Bureau (Library of Congress, 1909)

Second World War (1939–1945)

The Second World War resulted in the employment of approximately 300,000 disabled individuals. This employment was due to men and women leaving the private sector and working in government and martial jobs (Nielsen, 2012; Pelka, 2012, cited in Evans et al., 2017). As a result of being employed during this time, the disabled population's perceptions of themselves increased.

The public stopped viewing individuals with disabilities as insignificant; however, these same individuals, who were mostly from the armed forces, were now viewed as objects of pity and charity (Beilke and Yssel, 1999; Griffin et al., 2007; Imrie, 1997; Ward, 2009, cited in Evans et al., 2017).

On a personal note, I can relate to the above-mentioned statement. After my retinal detachments, I felt as though people were pitying me. Whenever I would speak to acquaintances or friends about my experiences, they would all look at me with the same commiserating expression. I felt like I was under a microscope examined and dissected one area at a time. It was as if my life was on full display, like I was some animal within a cage and people would pay and come to see me struggle to break free. The truth was I did not want to be pitied. I did not want to be viewed as a charity case. I just wanted to be understood, and I wanted someone to listen to me. Back then, I wanted to be seen as a person, not as my disability. I know that we have some more disability history to attend to; however, I felt that it was important to provide a personal perspective on the presented literature. Alright, shall we continue?

Serviceman's Readjustment Act

At this point, let us move to the year 1944. I know that you are probably thinking, "What is so special about 1944, Stephanie?" Well, I will tell you! In 1944, the Serviceman's Readjustment Act, also known as the GI Bill, was passed! This Bill was significant because it started a discussion regarding the mental and physical well-being of soldiers who had returned from the Second

World War. The GI Bill shed light on what American soldiers required to recuperate from the trauma that they had witnessed (McEnaney, 2011). So, what exactly did the GI Bill provide for soldiers who had returned from war? This Bill granted veterans one year of education if they had served in the military for 90 days. Additionally, veterans who were listed as single received $50.00 per month. Veterans who were married received $75.00 per month (Thelin, 2019). Overall, depending on the number of years veterans served their country, the GI Bill supplied $500.00 of education fees to those who attended "approved institutions" (Strom, 1950, cited in Madaus 2011, p. 6).

College and university campus reform

By the year 1946, veterans made up 52 percent of the American higher education population. Numerous enrolled veterans were disabled, and because they had specific needs, colleges and universities began establishing resource offices for disability support (Beilke and Yssel, 1999; Brown, 2008; Madaus, 2000, cited in Evans et al., 2017). Before the end of the Second World War, college and university campuses were inaccessible to physically disabled individuals (Madaus, 2000, cited in Evans et al., 2017). In 1948, Timothy Nugent established the first-ever higher education program for disabled individuals (University of Illinois Archives, 2017). Nugent, shown in Figure 5 (Kitch, 1952), was a veteran with disabilities. Additionally, he was a postsecondary student who was studying administration and psychology (Brown, 2008, cited in Evans et al., 2017). Known as "the Father of Accessibility," Nugent was a pioneer for those with physical disabilities (Chamberlain, 2024, p. 1). However, Nugent faced significant backlash from Adlai Stevenson, who was the governor of Illinois, and from the Galesburg administration. These individuals believed in their hearts that the University of Illinois' reputation would be based on its disabled student population rather than their academia. In 1949, Stevenson and Galesburg administrators shut down the campus (Brown, 2008, cited in Evans et al., 2017).

The program was moved to the University of Illinois' Urbana location because 14 students who used wheelchairs were granted 2 years of college education. At the time, they had only completed one year of their studies. After moving this program, Nugent worked diligently to make the new campus accessible. He installed ramps to six of the buildings that housed class-rooms, and he allowed the students to live in Second World War bases which had amenities such as a communal bathroom and ramps.

Nugent's advocacy efforts did not stop there. In addition to estab-lishing ramps for wheelchairs and "curb cuts," he also provided therapy services, disability-accessible transportation, a center for on-campus living for students with mobility disabilities, and the first-ever program where disabled students could study overseas (Brown, 2008, cited in Evans et al., 2017, p. 30). Figure 6 is an exam-ple of accessible transportation that was used at the University of Illinois campus (University of Illinois Archives, 1957).

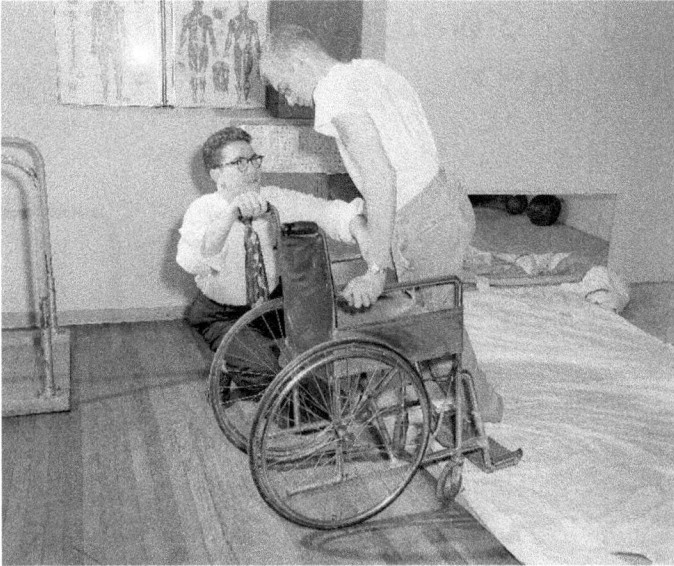

Figure 5. AP Photo/Edward Kitch, 1952

Figure 6. Student in Wheelchair Rides Blue Bull Bus, 1957 Courtesy of the University of Illinois Archives Found in RS 16/6/11, Box 4, Folder Transportation 1957

So, do you wanna start a revolution?

Advocating for the goals of the disability community and participating in activism help to change the disabled individual's perception of themselves and their disability (Smith and Mueller, 2022). Disability activism's roots are embedded in opposition to "the eugenics movement" (Evans et al., 2017, p. 33). The start of this movement began in 1880, and it continued until the Second World War came to an end. The sole belief regarding the term *eugenics* was that individuals with disabilities were degenerative and defective (Davis, 2006, cited in Evans et al., 2017). Disabled individuals rebelled against this disgusting movement, and this rebellion took the form of creating their own communal associations. In the nineteenth century, three communities were formed. The names of these communities were the National Association of the Deaf, the General Improvement Association, and the American Blind People's Higher Education Association (Kudlick, 2001; Longmore, 2009; Pelka, 2012, cited in Evans et al., 2017).

Crusaders of 1930s to the 1940s

As the infamous eugenics movement ended, individuals with disabilities were exhausted over the constant prejudice that they had endured during their lives. This community realized that they had had enough, and they were not going to take this horrific treatment any longer. It was at this pivotal moment that individuals with disabilities began to realize that they deserved better societal treatment (Neilsen, 2012, cited in Evans et. al., 2017). Multiple associations comprising individuals with disabilities began to fight for their rights for improved treatment and respect throughout the United States of America. After the Second World War, campaigners with physical disabilities directed their time and effort on their rights to attend institutions of higher education (Pelka, 2012, cited in Evans et al., 2017).

Disability in the 1950s

The 1950s were a time when additional universities were establishing programs for students with disabilities. See, Timothy Nugent, like Thomas Gallaudet, was another pioneer in the disability movement. Nugent truly set the foundation for disabled students' rights. Other universities that enacted similar programs include Florida State University, the University of Missouri, and Wayne State University. Unfortunately, these institutions were the exception to the rule. Many faculty and administrators still held this belief that supplying students who were severely disabled with a higher education degree was pointless. They figured that these individuals were not going to be successful in college nor were they going to acquire a job after graduating (Madaus, 2011, cited in Evans et al., 2017).

On a separate note, I believe that I just introduced you to ableism (i.e., disability discrimination). We will cover ableism in Chapter 4; however, the above-mentioned sentence is a prime example of what not to believe regarding those who have disabilities. I will always stand by the conviction that individuals with disabilities can be just as successful as those who are non-disabled. Remember, we are all human, and we are all worthy of success. Speaking of beliefs, I would now like to introduce you to activism within higher education. Individuals with disabilities fought relentlessly for their rights, and now it is the time to give them the proper respect and dignity that they deserve. With that, let us continue!

Change is coming: The 1960s to the 1970s

Activism was also prevalent on college and university campuses during the 1960s (Thelin, 2004, cited in Evans et al., 2017). Individuals began to criticize the medical model of disability, and they maintained that a social model be used to understand this phenomenon (Evans et al., 2017). The medical model portrays disability as insufficient, and this insufficiency is something that needs to be fixed. In contrast, the social model affirms that disabilities are just conditions of the body. It is not the individual who is disabled. Rather, the public is failing to assist a wide variety of needs at the intellectual, psychological, cognitive, and physical levels (Asch, 1998; Landsman, 2005; 2009; Smith, 2004; UPIAS, 1976, cited in Manago, Davis, and Goar, 2017). There were three federal laws that changed the trajectory for students with disabilities in higher education. I am so excited to explain these pieces of legislation to you!

Change is here: The Rehabilitation Act of 1973 (Section 504)

Before we get into the details surrounding Section 504, I would like to provide you with an interesting fact regarding the 37th president of the United States. During 1972, President Richard Nixon had rejected the Rehabilitation Act of 1973 not once, but

twice. In response to rejecting this important piece of legislation, organizational protests took place. The organizations that
actively protested this veto included the President's Committee
on the Employment of the Handicapped and Disabled in Action.
Finally, in 1973, President Nixon signed off on the third version
of the Rehabilitation Act that had been approved by Congress
(Longmore, 2003; Pelka, 2012, cited in Evans et al., 2017).

The Rehabilitation Act, specifically Section 504, was the initial legislation that provided protection to those with disabilities (*Title
II Subpart A of the Americans with Disabilities Act of 1990,* cited in
Murphy, 2021; Mueller and Broido, 2012). Section 504 states that
no disabled individual in the United States of America, on the
basis of their disability, shall be rejected from participating in, be
discriminated against, or be refused the benefits associated with
all programs or activities that receive assistance from Federal
funding (*Rehabilitation Act Section 504,* cited in Chamusco, 2017).
However, Section 504 only supplied a small amount of protection to individuals with disabilities. Disability rights advocates
were quite annoyed by this lack of protection (Chamusco, 2017).
Figure 7 shows a San Francisco 504 demonstration (Tusler, 1977).
The purpose of this protest was to regulate section 504 and to
ratify this federal law (Zinn Education Project, 2024a).

Despite this lack of protection, Section 504 of the Rehabilitation
Act of 1973 impelled institutions of higher education to deliver
assistance and accommodations to students with disabilities.
Some of the procedures and policies that pertain to this legislation are that higher education students need to ask for particular accommodation pertaining to their disability, and they must

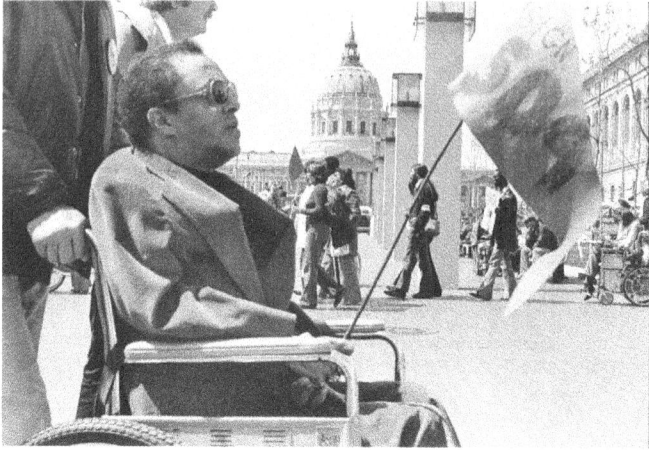

Figure 7. 1977 San Francisco 504 Demonstration Courtesy of Anthony Tusler

supply the necessary paperwork to on-campus disability special-ists that confirm their eligibility for accommodations (Madaus and Shaw, 2004).

A radical movement: The Americans with Disabilities Act of 1990

A remarkable breakthrough occurred 17 years later for all Americans with disabilities. It was July 26, 1990, when President George H.W. Bush signed the Americans with Disabilities Act into law. This federal legislation was revolutionary! The Americans with Disabilities Act, also known as the ADA, allowed disabled individ-uals to equally participate in activities and programs. Disability discrimination was forbidden in every aspect of communal life (ADA National Network, 2015; *Section 504 of the Rehabilitation Act of 1973*, cited in Murphy, 2021).

The Americans with Disabilities Act, specifically Title II, was significantly impactful within the context of public higher education. Title II protects students with disabilities from inequitable treatment by institutions that were supplied state funding. Furthermore, the ADA authorizes that American colleges and universities must supply accommodations to students with disabilities so that they may be given equitable chances within public higher education institutions (Holt et al., 2019). It is also worth mentioning that community colleges and occupational institutions are also protected by Title II of the ADA. Now, we cannot forget about private institutions. Private colleges and universities are protected by the ADA; however, their protection falls under Title III of this federal law (ADA National Network, 2024). Despite this necessary protection, there are some drawbacks to this law.

Under the ADA, students with disabilities must willingly self-identify to acquire the appropriate disability accommodations (Aquino and Bittinger, 2019). A trend in the literature shows that higher education students who possess disabilities fail to request the necessary accommodations which they require to be successful. There are a multitude of reasons as to why college and university students fail to request accommodations, and this topic is something that we will further explore in Chapters 2 and 4.

An additional drawback of the ADA was that limitations were placed on terminology such as *practical accommodation* and *disability* by a conservative Supreme Court. To address these inconsistencies, the Americans with Disabilities Amendments Act of 2008 (ADAAA) was established (Evans et al., 2017). Now, before I provide you with an explanation of the ADAAA, I would like to introduce you to a significant event surrounding the Americans with Disabilities Act of 1990. This event is called the "Capitol Crawl" (Zinn Education Project, 2024b, p. 1). We will also discuss the Higher Education Opportunity Act of 2008.

The Capitol Crawl of 1990

During the winter of 1990, the United States Congress delayed the passing of the ADA pertaining to its transportation and "public works" section (Zinn Education Project, 2024b, p. 1). Transportation is covered under Title II of the ADA (Disability Rights North Carolina, 2021). In response to the stalling of the ADA, disability advocates and those from the disabled community began to protest in Washington, D.C. On March 12, 1990, activists deserted their aids for mobility, and they started to crawl up the United States Capitol Building steps (Zinn Education Project, 2024b). One of the most notorious crawlers was Jennifer Keelan who was only eight years old (Skudra, 2023). Congress was required to respond to the protests. The ADA was finally passed through the Senate and the House of Representatives (Zinn Education Project, 2024b).

More change: The Higher Education Opportunity Act of 2008

Prior to the amendment of the American with Disabilities Act of 1990, the Higher Education Opportunity Act (HEOA) was established on August 14, 2008. This federal law renewed the Higher Education Act of 1965 (U.S. Department of Education, 2023). The HEOA provides descriptions of programs for students with disabilities so that they may obtain a high-quality college or university education (Madaus, Kowitt, and Lalor, 2012). Most notably, this federal law focused on providing instructional material that is accessible, and it sought to expand and evaluate access on the basis of equality. For example, the HEOA enacted "the Advisory Commission on Accessible Instructional Materials in Postsecondary Education for Students with Disabilities" (Evans et al., 2017, pp. 99–100). The purpose of establishing this commission was to find solutions for students who experienced challenges pertaining to print disabilities (Evans, 2008, cited in Evans et al., 2017).

You are probably asking yourselves, "What is a print disability?" Well, a print disability is a physical, visual, developmental, intellectual, perceptual, or learning disability that inhibits an individual from reading typical print (Centre for Equitable Library Access, 2024; Perkins School for the Blind, 2023). Some of the human conditions connected to print disabilities include autism, visual impairments, including low vision and/or blindness, brain injuries, and learning disabilities (Perkins School for the Blind, 2023).

Providing clarity: The Americans with Disabilities Amendments Act of 2008

We are now back to the ADA! The Americans with Disabilities Act of 1990 was a momentous milestone for individuals with disabilities. There is no denying that fact. However, how disability was legally interpreted was strict in nature, and individuals with substantial disabilities were rejected from obtaining protection from this federal law. These restrictions substantially impacted students with disabilities in higher education. For example, two court of appeals stated that college students who possessed learning disabilities were unable to obtain ADA protection (*Singh v. George Washington University School of Medicine and Health Services*, 2007; *Wong v. Regents of the University of California*, 2005, cited in Keenan et al., 2019). To give you some insight as to how serious this situation was, I would like to provide you with a definition of the term *learning disability*. According to the National Institute of Neurological Disorders and Stroke (NINDS):

"Learning disabilities are disorders that affect the ability to:

- Understand or use spoken or written language
- Do mathematical calculations
- Coordinate movements
- Direct attention" (NINDS, 2023, p. 1).

Given the struggles that these students endured within their higher education institutions, it was essential that they be provided with the necessary protection that was due to them under the ADA. Under the original ratification of this federal law, these students were not going to be protected. All of this changed on September 25, 2008, when President George W. Bush signed the Americans with Disabilities Amendments Act into law (Rozalski et al., 2010). The ADAAA supplied a comprehensive definition of the term *disability* (Keenan et al., 2019). This federal law sustained the original definition of disability. Under this definition, a disability is an impairment that substantially constrains one or "major life activities," a record that documents the impairment or being deemed as having the impairment (U.S. Department of Labor,

2009, p. 2). However, one of the biggest changes associated with this law was an extended list of what constituted significant life activities (Keenan et al., 2019; U.S. Department of Labor, 2009). As far as higher education was concerned, components such as thinking, reading, learning, and communication fell under the category of significant life activities. The ADAAA also applied to the brain and the nervous system (Keenan et al., 2019).

Disability history: Final thoughts

Many individuals with disabilities spent a lifetime fighting for their rights. They wanted to be seen, to be heard, and to be respected. They wanted nothing more than to show the world that they had the right to equitable treatment. Let the history of disability within higher education be a lesson for us to do better, and to not make the same mistakes that were made in the past. At this point, the questions that we must ask ourselves are the following: How is disability viewed by college and university educators today? What is the overall campus climate for students who have disabilities? What resources are offered to these students so that they may succeed in higher education? These questions will be answered in the next chapter. Off we go!

2
Disability within higher education today

Before we explore the current higher education landscape for students with disabilities, I want to provide you with some important facts that you should keep in mind as we move forward in this chapter. Colleges and universities have observed an increased quantity of students with disabilities registering within their higher education institutions. This has increased over a 30-year period (Blasey, Wang, and Blasey, 2023). Statistically speaking, in 2011–2012, 11 percent of undergraduate students stated that they had a disability (Snyder et al., 2016, cited in U.S. Department of Education, 2017, p. 1). Fast forward to 2019–2020, according to the National Center for Education Statistics (n.d.), approximately 21 percent of undergraduate and 11 percent of graduate students affirmed that they had a disability (p. 1). So, during a span of eight to ten years, the percentage of undergraduate students with a disability enrolling within higher education institutions increased by ten percent! This is a significant increase!

From an undergraduate standpoint

In addition to the above-mentioned statistics, I want you to have a general idea of the types of disabilities that are often reported by higher education students. The American College Health Association (ACHA) examined 54,000 undergraduates in 2022. Below are the findings from this survey. To spice things up a bit, I decided to create a bar graph to illustrate these results. Please refer to Figure 8 (American College Health Association, 2022, cited in Welding, 2023; Levin, 2024) for this masterpiece.

Despite the lovely illustration that I have provided, let us high-light some key statistics within the bar graph. The bar graph

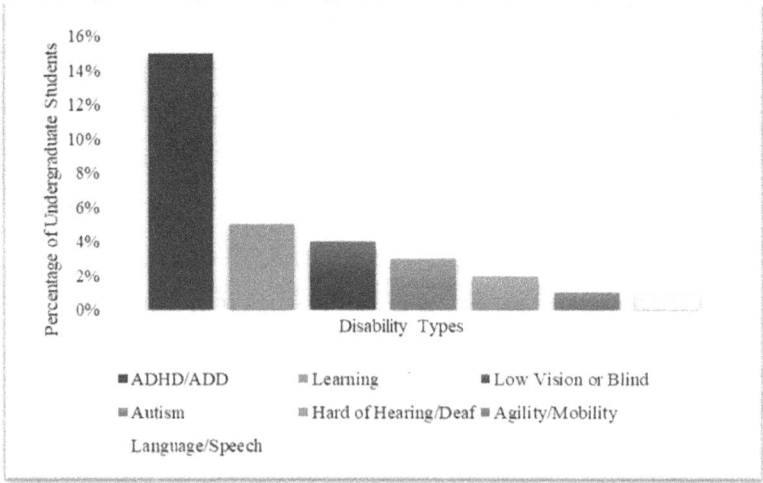

Figure 8. Disabilities Reported by Higher Education Students

Source: The American College Health Association, 2022, cited in Welding, 2023. Bar chart was created by Stephanie Levin (2024).

shows that 15 percent of undergraduate students stated that they had attention deficit disorder or attention deficit hyperactivity disorder, 5 percent of undergraduate students possessed a learning disability, 4 percent of these students either possessed low vision, or were blind, and 3 percent were on the autism spectrum (ACHA, 2022, cited in Welding, 2023, p. 3).

Mental health concerns

Mental health issues are also prevalent on college and university campuses. During spring 2023, it was reported that 53 percent of undergraduate students had met the standards associated with loneliness, 31 percent met the standards for suicidal ideation, and 3 percent of undergraduate students attempted suicide during the last year. Additionally, 8 percent of higher education students had received a diagnosis of post-traumatic stress disorder or other disorder associated with trauma, 36 percent of these students had anxiety, and 28 percent had depression (ACHA, 2023, cited in Bryant and Welding, 2024, pp. 3–4).

As you read this book, I want you to keep in mind the data associated with students who are blind or possess low vision as well as the mental health statistics associated with anxiety, depression, post-traumatic stress disorder, and suicidal ideation. It is important that you remember this information for two reasons:

- Once we get to Chapter 3, we are going to focus heavily on visual impairments. The first two chapters are intended to introduce you to disability within higher education. I believe that for you to understand what it means to be visually impaired in a college or university setting, I need to provide you with a foundational understanding of disability.

- At the beginning of this book, I have provided you with a content warning where I will discuss my mental health struggles associated with being visually impaired. The truth is, I went through some extremely dark times during those experiences, and although I have come out on the other side, it took me years to overcome my demons. To be honest, I still have lingering mental health effects because of what I had endured. Although the aforementioned mental health statistics are from a general standpoint, it is important that you remember them because in Chapter 6, these topics are going to pop up again from a visual impairment point of view.

From a graduate standpoint

Although there has been an uptick in the number of students with disabilities entering colleges and universities which, by the way, is great news, this community endures increased rates of dropout, substandard academic outcomes, and prolonged amounts of time to finish their degrees (Adams and Proctor, 2010; Koch et al., 2018; Newman et al., 2011, cited in Blasey, Wang, and Blasey, 2023). In 2011, approximately 49.5 percent of students with disabilities who registered at a four-year institution finished their bachelor's degrees during a six-year period. In contrast, 68 percent of non-disabled students completed their degrees during this time frame (Welding, 2023, p. 6). An additional analysis took place in 2023 which examined data from the United States Census. Almost 20 percent of disabled individuals aged 25–34 years old possessed a bachelor's degree or had attained a higher educational degree. The percentage of non-disabled individuals who possessed a bachelor's degree or a higher degree was 41 percent. Despite this substantial difference, there is some good news! Between 2008 and 2021, the percentage of individuals with disabilities who are getting their bachelor's degrees doubled (Welding, 2023, p. 6).

Current view of disabilities within higher education

To fully understand disabilities within higher education today, it is essential that we go back to 1973. In Chapter 1, we discussed the Rehabilitation Act of 1973. Under the Rehabilitation Act, higher education students attending public colleges and universities could not be rejected due to their disability. Within the realm of higher education, either accommodations would be put into effect that were not previously granted to students with disabilities, or the availability of these accommodations was unsystematic. No uniform standards of accessibility existed for these students, and it was important that the United States Government create a widespread system for educational access. So, what do you think happened next? In 1978, the National Council on Disability Education (NCD) was established! Originally, the NCD acted as a consultative board to the Department of Education; however, during 1984, the National Council on Disability Education began to act as a separate entity. Independent of the Department of Education, the NCD's responsibilities included evaluating all national policies and programs for disabilities. This supervision was further expanded outside the realm of education (NCD, 2013, cited in Oslund, 2015). Legally, there was a prioritized increase for students who had disabilities to demand access to their educations; however, institutions of education were unclear as to how they were supposed to supply their students with these services. Institutions realized that there was a need for a primary individual to establish and institute accessible standards for students with disabilities. Suppliers of these services understood that they needed to keep having conversations about what constituted "best practices" (Oslund, 2015, p. 63). There also needed to be discussions regarding legal matters pertaining to disability, and disability educational resources had to be established for individuals providing disability services (Oslund, 2015). As a result, AHEAD was enacted.

AHEAD

In 1977, the Association on Higher Education and Disability® (AHEAD) was created for the purpose of sharing practices, resources, and information (Oslund, 2015). AHEAD is specifically for professionals who are dedicated to providing a friendly post-secondary environment for individuals with disabilities. These resources are marketed towards Student Affairs staff, providers of disability services, and officers of diversity. AHEAD promotes networking among members and communities; provides opportunities to develop professionally through workshops, conferences, and publications; and notifies associates of developing problems applicable to higher education and disability at the legislative level. As of 2024, AHEAD is comprised of over 5,000 members (AHEAD, 2024). In addition, please see Figure 9 for a photo of the 2019 AHEAD conference (Spears, 2019).

Figure 9. Valerie Spears, AHEAD

Disability support offices

This next section begs the following question to be answered: What is it that disability support offices and disability services professionals do? Let us begin by addressing the role of disability support offices. Due to the enactment of the Americans with Disabilities Act of 1990, institutions of higher education must safeguard "equal access" to students who have disabilities. To guarantee this access, on-campus amenities must be physically accessible, and educational accommodations such as time extensions on tests and interpreters of sign language must be supplied to students with disabilities (ADA, 1990; Forsbach and Rice-Mason, 2001, cited in Kim, 2021, p. 167). There is a significant difference between support at the primary, secondary, and postsecondary levels. Within the context of primary and secondary education, support for students with disabilities is legally ensured. However, according to the ADA, higher education students must self-identify and state that they have a disability. In addition, students with disabilities need to actively request services and support, and they need to supply evidence to establish how their disability hinders them from participating in significant life events (Adreon and Durocher, 2007, cited in Kim, 2021; Miller, Lewandowski, and Antshel, 2015, cited in Weis and Bittner, 2022). The majority of disability support offices supply information pertaining to the types of services that they provide. Also, disability support offices advise students with disabilities about the required paperwork to qualify for accommodations as well as the process for obtaining the necessary accommodations (Kim, 2021). To provide you with some insight into the types of accommodations that are available to students with disabilities, I have compiled a short list of some of these services:

- Early registration time
- Larger print
- Notetaker (This is either by recording or by another person. I had the option to use a notetaker within my classes.)
- Service animal
- Breaktime during exams
- Interpreter of American Sign Language (Rutgers-New Brunswick Office of Disability Services, 2024a).

In addition to the accommodations that are commonly provided by disability support offices, below is an example of the steps that students need to take when registering for their accommodations:

1. Students who need accommodations should contact the Office of Accessibility Services either when a disability

has been identified or they have been accepted to the university.

2. The student needs to supply essential documentation that supports the disability. Documentation varies based on the type of disability.

3. Once the student provides the required documentation, they will meet with the coordinator of accessibility services. At this stage, the student will have a meeting with a staff member of Accessibility Services where they will discuss the student's accommodations and create a plan. In addition, all students requesting accommodations must attend a workshop so that they may complete the registration process and acquire accommodations.

4. If a student needs accommodations in the classroom, faculty are automatically notified via an automatic letter. However, it is expected that the student speaks with the faculty member as soon as the accommodations are sent out (Rowan University Office of Accessibility Services, 2024).

Professionals of disability services

Disability services professionals have multiple responsibilities. These responsibilities include the following:

*   Guaranteeing that the essential supports and services are supplied to students with disabilities.
*   Supervising the campus for accessibility purposes.
*   Meeting and reviewing disability documentation with students.
*   Collaborating with the student on what resources are needed for success and access within their academic careers.

Disability services professionals also collaborate with a diverse range of individuals within the public and the campus community (Oslund, 2015). For example, these individuals provide orientations, staff and faculty retreats, and information assemblies for new employees. Additional programs and services that are provided by disability services professionals include organizing disability seminars, having guest speakers present at their institutions, and holding movie nights. Professionals who are active within the context of disability hold outreach programs that assist high school students in learning about the different services that are offered to students with disabilities (Lalor, Madaus, and Newman, 2020). Disability services' assistance does not stop there. In fact, some colleges and universities hold programs that assist students with disabilities in transitioning to university campus life. By participating in these programs, students are able to move into their campus housing early, participate in personal tours of the campus, and further participate in activities during the welcome week (Rowan University Office of Accessibility Services, 2024).

Failure to request accommodations

Although disability services professionals are working to provide an all-inclusive environment, students are still failing to request accommodations. I have found that there are multiple reasons as to why students do not request accommodations. In fact, in March 2024, I had written an opinion piece titled *Many Students Don't Inform Their Colleges about Their Disability. That Needs to*

Change in response to this issue. As stated in Chapter 1, the Americans with Disabilities Act prohibits college and university campuses from pursuing the disability statuses of their students. Due to this restriction, students with disabilities need to act as self-advocates, and they are responsible for requesting their own accommodations (Blasey, Wang, and Blasey. 2023). This process brings forth multiple obstacles for disabled students. These challenges include a lack of knowledge associated with the self-identification process and the resources that are available to the student (Blasey, Wang, and Blasey, 2023; Lehrer-Stein and Berger, 2023). However, stigma is the most common reason for students not requesting accommodations (Levin, 2024b).

Disability stigma is quite complex, and unfortunately, as a visually impaired women, I, too, have had the utmost privilege of experiencing this type of stigma. I say that statement with sarcasm because disability stigma is not something that you want to experience. If anything, I wish that I could have avoided that experience altogether. Yet, if I had not endured this type of stigma and not experienced my own disability, I would not have had the opportunity to write this book. Most importantly, I would not have had the pleasure of meeting you and helping you understand what it is to have a disability within higher education. As I often tell myself, everything happens for a reason. We may not know exactly what that reason is, but, rest assured, the answer will eventually reveal itself in time. On that note, we will revisit disability stigma in Chapter 4, and I will provide you with my story on how I experienced stigma from friends, acquaintances, partners, and a former professor of mine.

Do I really belong?

John Clifford was a screenplay writer for a movie titled *Carnival of Souls* (Kenneth Spencer Research Library Archival Collections, n.d.). In this movie, there is a quote that really stuck with me. It says the following:

> I don't belong in this world. That's what it is. Something separates me from other people. (John Clifford, 1962, cited in BrainyQuote, 2024, p. 1).

This quote is impactful, and it made me think about how students with disabilities experience lower senses of belonging within their higher education institutions. In fact, in 2021, the National Center for College Students with Disabilities published a research brief with significant findings. Out of 54,000 students who were surveyed, students with disabilities reported feeling a decreased sense of belonging as compared to students who did not have disabilities. In addition to experiencing lower senses of belonging, students with disabilities have endured increased levels of on-campus discrimination (Soria, 2021, cited in Welding, 2023, p. 10). Some forms of on-campus discrimination that students with disabilities experience include stereotypes, insults, or "physical attacks" (U.S. Department of Education, n.d. p. 7).

Disability in higher education today: Final feelings and thoughts

We have arrived at the end of Chapter 2! Thank you so much for sticking with me for this long! Within this chapter, we have covered the current landscape of disability within higher education. We have learned so much in such a short time, and I am happy to report that we are not yet finished with our journey. In our next chapter, we are going to jump to a completely different topic. This chapter is what I would like to call the reason for writing this book. Here, we are going to delve into the realm of visual impairments. In this chapter, we are going to define the term *visual impairment*, and we are going to discuss the multiple conditions that cause visual impairments to occur.

3
Visual impairment: A definition and overview

There is no single definition that perfectly defines the term *visual impairment*. To tell the truth, there are a multitude of definitions that exist for this terminology. Personally, I like to keep things simple. So, for this book, we are going to use the following definition:

> Visual impairment is defined as when individuals experience any form of vision loss.
> This statement applies to a person who either has some vision loss or who is unable to see at all. (Salvin, 2016)

From a global standpoint, no less than 2.2 billion individuals have a nearsighted or farsighted visual impairment. At a minimum, 1 billion, or approximately half, of these visual impairment cases are either not addressed or could have been stopped (World Health Organization, 2023b, p. 1). Nationally speaking, over 1.6 million Americans who are blind or who are existing with vision loss are under 40 years old (CDC, 2024c, p. 2). Before we delve into some of the typical forms of vision loss, I want to talk about the characteristics that are often associated with having visual impairments.

Visual impairment characteristics

When a person has a visual impairment, there are a few components to keep in mind. Some of the typical characteristics associated with being visually impaired include the following:

- Sensitivity to light: Discomfort or pain can occur when exposed to bright lights
- Tunnel vision: Occurs when an individual is unable to see objects from below, above, or the side of their central field of vision
- Blurry vision: When objects look out of focus or blurred
- Blindness at night: When an individual has a hard time adapting to dim or low light
- Decreased visual sharpness: Occurs when an individual has a tough time seeing objects up closely (Besser Eye Care Team, 2023).

You know, it is funny. As I was writing the aforementioned paragraph, I could not help but begin to have flashbacks of my own experiences. That first characteristic, sensitivity to light, is all too familiar to me. After my first eye surgery, which was during the thick of summer, I could not even walk outside because my eyes were so sensitive to light. Back then, I was still wearing glasses, so I had to wear these sunglasses that fit over my regular eyeglasses. I cringe as I think about those sunglasses. They made me feel so hideous, and when I wore them, I felt like I was older than my time. My eyes were even more sensitive to light after my second surgery. After I was able to safely wear my contact lenses, I purchased a pair of oversized, UV-protectant sunglasses. They were super cute, and I loved wearing them. I loved wearing them so much that the very thought of removing them resulted in me having anxiety-induced panic attacks. The idea of actually removing my sunglasses outside was terrifying to me because I was able to see the vision loss and floaters that affected both of my eyes. Because of this fear, as soon as I left my house, my sunglasses went on my face. Over time, I began to wear my sunglasses inside because sometimes the lighting would continue to affect my eyes. I felt safer indoors, but the sunglasses acted as my security blanket. Please refer to Figure 10 for my photo wearing sunglasses while on vacation for my 23rd birthday (Levin, 2015).

Figure 10. Me wearing my sunglasses in June 2015, six months after my second retinal detachment surgery. Photo taken by Stephanie Levin (2015)

Please do not let this picture of me fool you. On the outside, you see a happy, smiling young woman who is celebrating her birthday in Walt Disney World. What you do not see is the fear that I felt in taking off my sunglasses, or the sadness that plagued me on a daily basis as I was mourning the loss of my Grandmom. You do not see how hard I was trying to appear "normal" to everyone, or the tears that I had shed during that trip. There is no indication of a shattered self-esteem. But, beneath the surface, I can assure you, all of those feelings and emotions are there.

Blurry vision was another constant presence in my life. The gas bubble that was placed to flatten the retina in my right eye resulted in vision distortion. I could not see anything except for the texture of the bubble. Shortly after my surgery, I tried to help my mom unload the dishwasher. At the time, I felt like all I was good at was taking up space, so to feel useful, I attempted to help my mom complete a simple chore. While I was walking to the hutch to put the plates away, they suddenly dropped out of my hands. As they began crashing down on the floor, I stood there with a mix of bewilderment and embarrassment. Although the plates were plastic, and they did not break, I felt like I did not have any control over my body. I looked down at the floor at the plates, and then I looked at my mom. I did this a few times until I finally burst into tears.

Forms of visual impairment

While there are so many ways to define the term *visual impairment*, there are also different conditions that cause visual impairment. I am not going to provide you with an extensive list of every single type of visual impairment known to human beings. Instead,

I want to briefly highlight some of the typical visual impairments that you will most likely see at some point during your lives.

Amblyopia

Amblyopia, also known as lazy eye, is decreased vision in a person's eye. This condition is caused by irregular development of their vision. The eye that is affected by amblyopia turns outward or inward. Development of this condition occurs from the time that an individual is born to age seven. It is rare that both eyes are affected by amblyopia (Mayo Clinic Staff, 2021). Figure 11 shows an illustration of what amblyopia looks like (Cooke, 2021).

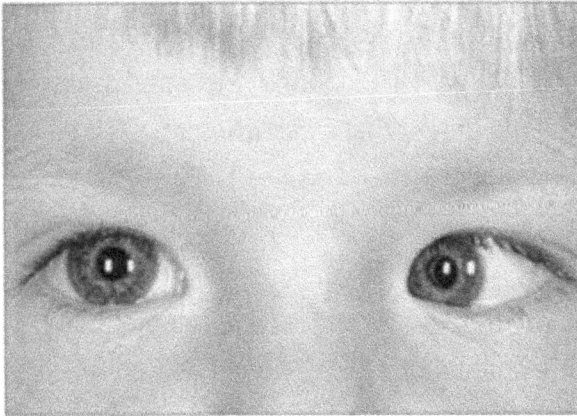

Figure 11. Amblyopia

Courtesy of Dr. Kyle Cooke, O.D. (2021).

Aniridia

Aniridia, which is illustrated in Figure 12 (Cahoon and Pettey, 2016), is characterized by a complete or partially absent iris. A person can either be born with this condition, or they can acquire it later on in life (Tripathy and Salini, 2023).

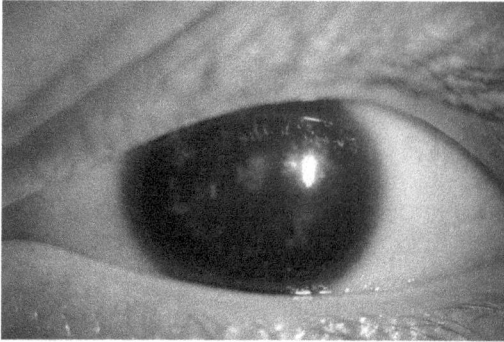

Figure 12. Congenital Aniridia

Courtesy of Judd Cahoon, PhD and Dr. Jeff Pettey, MD (2016)

Albinism

Albinism is a rare, genetic condition that occurs when a person is born without the typical amount of melanin. Essentially, melanin is defined as a pigment that establishes an individual's hair color, eye color, and skin tone. Melanin is also a component in the development of the optic nerve. Basically, this pigment assists in the normal functioning of the eye. From a visual standpoint, albinism can result in rapid eye movement, crossed eyes, issues with depth perception, and vision that is distorted or blurry (Cleveland Clinic, 2024).

Blindness

Blindness is when either a person is unable to see or their field of vision is lacking. There are different types of blindness. There is low or partial blindness where an individual still has some vision. Another form of blindness, inherited blindness, is defined as when a person is born with vision issues such as conditions of the retina, uninherited birth defects, and eye issues. Then you have legal blindness, which is characterized as having 20/200 vision even when using contact lenses or glasses. A person who is affected by legal blindness needs to be ten times nearer to an object, or, in order to see an object, it needs to be ten times bigger. Legal blindness also applies to individuals whose peripheral or field of vision is significantly decreased. Finally, a person can be completely blind. This rare condition is when an individual is unable to notice or see light (Cleveland Clinic, 2022a).

Cataracts

Cataracts occur when the eye's lens becomes cloudy. Some of the symptoms of cataracts include blurry vision, difficulty seeing people and objects at night, double vision within one eye, and light and glare sensitivity. Additionally, if you have cataracts, you will mostly likely see "halos around lights" (Mayo Clinic Staff, 2022a, p. 2). After I had undergone my second retinal detachment surgery, I developed a cataract in my right eye. I was young, and when someone young has experienced eye surgeries, the chances of them developing a cataract are extremely high. Also, because my left eye was lasered to prevent a retinal detachment from occurring, a small cataract developed in that eye as well. Let me be clear and say that cataracts are extremely annoying. They gradually get worse over time, and it gets to a point where you are unable to see anything. Colors no longer appear vibrant and beautiful, and it is true that halos begin to form around lights. Cataracts can significantly impact your quality of life, and they need to be removed when they are fully mature. I will describe my experiences with cataracts in more detail in Chapter 7. In the meantime, please refer to Figure 13 for an illustration of what

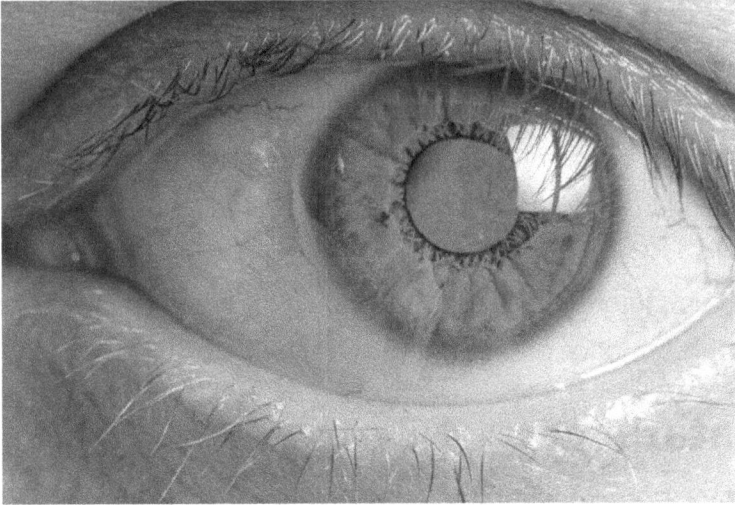

Figure 13. Cataract clouding of the lens of the human eye

Credit: iStock.com/Zarina Lukash (2021)

a human eye's lens looks like when a cataract is developing (Lukash, 2021).

Color blindness

Color blindness, also known as "color vision deficiency," is defined as when an individual views colors in a different manner than the majority of people. This condition makes it challenging for individuals to recognize differences between particular colors (National Eye Institute, 2024a, p. 1).

Glaucoma

Glaucoma is an eye disease that occurs when fluid accumulates within the frontal part of a person's eye. This fluid buildup results in optic nerve damage and increased eye pressure (Boyd,

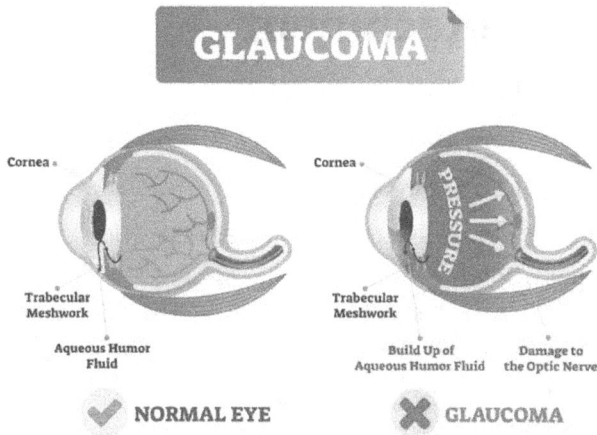

Figure 14. Glaucoma illness vector illustration. Cross-section close-up comparison with normal and damaged eye. Scheme with cornea, trabecular meshwork, aqueous humor fluid, pressure, and optic nerve damage stock illustration

Credit: iStock.com/VectorMine (2018)

McKinney, and Turbert, 2023). Figure 14 shows the difference between a healthy eye and an eye that has been affected by glaucoma (VectorMine, 2018).

Hyperopia

Hyperopia is the opposite of myopia. I am extremely myopic which means that I am severely nearsighted. To put it into perspective, before I had an intraocular lens placed in my right eye after cataract removal surgery, my vision was -13. Currently, I am -10 in my left eye, and I wear a contact lens in that eye during the day. So, to have hyperopia is to be farsighted, or to have an easier time seeing objects that are further away (American Optometric Association, n.d.).

Retinal detachment

I know that I had discussed what retinal detachment is in the introduction of my book. Instead of providing you with another explanation of this eye disorder, I want to show you what my vision currently looks like today. Please see Figure 15 for this illustration (Levin, 2024).

The black portions of my eye represent vision loss. My second detachment ended up going into the central part of my field of vision which resulted in me losing some of my sight. As you can see, I have vision loss in the left, upper, and lower areas of my right eye. In the beginning, my vision loss was incredibly frustrating. My brain had not yet adjusted to my new field of vision, so the vision loss was very noticeable. The presence of this vision loss only further exacerbated my anxiety, and every time I saw the damage, I kept thinking that my retina was detaching again. Over time, my brain compensated for this change, and the vision loss is not as noticeable as it was before. The damage within the left portion of my eye is consistent; however, the damage within

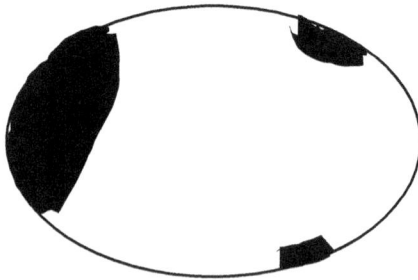

Figure 15. My right-eye vision. Image created by Stephanie Levin (2024e)

the upper and lower portions of my eye tends to show up when I am experiencing stress, or when I am focusing on these areas for long periods of time. Sometimes, the vision loss within the lower right portion of my eye shows up as a flash of light.

As far as my left eye is concerned, my retina specialist lasered it to prevent my retina from detaching, so I have not experienced a retinal detachment in that eye. However, because I am severely myopic, I have persistent, clear floaters in my left eye. The floaters can be quite a nuisance, and they are most noticeable on cloudy days. For this reason, you will often see me wearing my sunglasses even when it is not sunny outside. In addition to the ever-present floaters, the surgeries have left both of my eyes more sensitive to light.

Essentially, one of the primary characteristics of a retinal detachment is a big, black curtain or shadow that is located within the middle of a person's vision. This shadow or curtain can also be located within a person's peripheral vision (National Eye Institute, 2024b).

Visual impairments: Closing comments

We are at the end of Chapter 3! Now, you have a basic understanding of what it means to have visual impairments and the different types of visual impairments that exist. Let us move on to Chapter 4, where we will discuss disability stigma and ableism within higher education. I will also tell you my story of how I endured this type of stigma as a higher education student.

4
Disability stigma: The never-ending cycle

I was thinking of a clever way to begin this chapter. As you can probably tell by reading the introduction of this book, I love music. I feel that the lyrics of a song can speak to any significant moment of our lives. So, when I think about stigma and disability, I equate this phenomenon to Bernard Rothman's (1988) lyrical masterpiece *The Song That Never Ends*. You see, disability stigma is truly a never-ending cycle. It is an uphill battle that we, the visually impaired community, have to face on an everyday basis. When I endured disability stigma, I found myself trying to over-compensate for my limitations. In my mind, I had to outperform everyone in my classes. I needed to put on a brave face for all of the world to see, and I had to show my friends, family, professors, and acquaintances that my disability did not define me. As I reflect back on that period of my life, all I can remember is how much I wanted other people to see me as a person. While there were some individuals who showed me kindness during and after my surgeries, there were other people who, after looking at me, could only see my impairment. To be honest, as I had explained in Chapter 1, there were moments when I felt like a walking charity case rather than a human being. When I explained my surgeries to some people, I would see their expressions, and I could only imagine what they must have been thinking. Their eyes said the following: "Oh, poor Steph, she has been through so much! She just can't catch a break!" Pity is truly a wonderful thing, is it not? The truth is pity is not a wonderful thing. What is truly wonderful is treating others with decency, and not making judgments based on their disabilities. Remember, individuals with visual impairments are capable of everything and anything, and it is time that we started to believe that statement. So, let me formally begin this chapter by providing you with an understanding of disability stigma. Also, I want to take a moment to talk about ableism. I know that I had briefly introduced you to ableism in Chapter 1; however, I think that you need to be provided with a deeper understanding of this concept.

What is disability stigma?

The term *stigma* is derived from the Greek word *mark*. From a general standpoint, stigma pertains to the negative points of view regarding other individuals who have certain qualities (Healthy Aging RRTC, n.d.). Essentially, stigma relates to experiencing everyday life with an undervalued, societal identity. Disability is one of the many qualities that is devalued within the public (Goffman, 1963, cited in Partow, Cook, and McDonald, 2021). In terms of higher education, the stigma that students with disabilities endure might be influenced by the perceptions of able-bodied individuals (Zhou, 2023). Moreover, the stigmatization or negative points of view that are directed at individuals with disabilities are considered undetectable barriers that influence societal inequities. These inequities include differences in post-secondary registration and completion of one's college degree (Bogart et al., 2019). Below are some ways that disability stigma can be portrayed. This list is not exclusive. Rather, I am going to discuss the forms of disability stigma that I had experienced in higher education. These types of stigma include the following:

- Stereotypes: It is assumed that individuals with disabilities cannot take care of themselves, or they are dependent on other people

- Condescending behavior: Individuals with disabilities are victims of overprotection, and they find themselves being babied by other people

- Discrimination: Individuals with disabilities might not be granted certain opportunities due to stereotypes and assumptions regarding their disability

- Internalizing: Individuals who possess a disability might experience shame, embarrassment, or pessimistic view-points pertaining to their disability

- Suppression: Individuals with disabilities hide their impairments within mainstream society (Healthy Aging RRTC, n.d.).

What is ableism?

Ableism is defined as adverse prejudice and attitudes that are geared towards a person according to their status of disability (Fierros, 2006, cited in Lett, Tamaian, and Klest, 2020). What is the one component that keeps this type of prejudice alive?

The answer is simple: Bias. It is bias that perpetuates favoritism towards non-disabled individuals. Bias also supports inequitable institutional practices or structures. This inequity applies to universities as well (Beratan, 2006; Kattari, 2017, cited in Lett, Tamaian, and Klest, 2020). Some common forms of ableism that individuals with visual impairments experience include:

- Speaking to adults or teenagers who have disabilities in a patronizing or childlike manner
- Presuming that a person's life is based around their disability and that they are incapable of having other responsibilities and goals
- Ridiculing or humiliating a person for having a disability

(Perkins School for the Blind, 2024).

Disability stigma and ableism are persistent problems within higher education and society as a whole. These forms of degradation are pervasive, and, like weeds, they grow larger and longer because they are cultivated through hatred, small-mindedness, and microaggressions. In the next section of this chapter, I want to share multiple moments throughout my retinal detachment journey where I experienced stigma and ableism. These events are not meant to be listed in chronological order. Rather, this is an opportunity for you to understand how ableism and stigma are realistically portrayed. Yes, the events below did occur, and yes, they brought me a lot of pain. However, I am choosing to use these moments as teachable experiences so that we do not keep making the same mistakes pertaining to stigma and ableism over and over again.

My experiences with ableism and stigma

Class is in session

One moment that really stands out to me is when I experienced stigma and ableism within my college of choice. In spring 2014, I was taking four of my core business classes for my undergraduate degree. One of my capstone classes entailed a lot of time on the computer, and to be honest, the courseload was quite heavy. For these reasons, I ended up dropping that class. One day, I was walking in the hall of my university, and I saw the professor of this class. I ran up to him, and I explained that the reason that I had dropped his course was because I had undergone eye surgery to repair a retinal detachment, and I could not go for extensive periods of time looking at a computer screen. As we were walking, he said to me, "Well, you better get used to it. That is what college is, looking at screens." At the time, his comment had not registered. Maybe it was a mixture of shock and surprise? What I can tell you is that I was taken aback by his statement, and I did not know how to respond. How does one even respond to a statement like that? To this day, I cannot believe that he could be so cold and uncaring. The lack of empathy regarding my circumstances was astounding.

Friends forever?

My experiences associated with ableism and stigma did not end there. In college, I had many friends. Some were extremely supportive of my condition, and I cannot begin to tell you how grateful I am for their friendship. They are true friends who have stuck by me during the good times and the bad. However, I had other friends who did not fully understand my impairment. One night, I was speaking to a friend of mine on the phone. At the time, I was explaining to him that I could not drive because of the side effects from my first surgery. Additionally, I was terrified of driving again. My eyes were not in good shape, and I really did not feel comfortable getting behind the wheel. I explained this to my friend, he said to me, "Your parents can't drive you around forever." As I held onto the phone with my mouth agape, I was overcome with a surge of shame and embarrassment. My stomach twinged with anxiety, and my face grew hot, and red. I felt so ashamed of my disability. I asked myself if he was truly a friend. At the time, I thought that he was. Now, I am not so sure. True friends stick by you through thick and thin. Obviously, my "friend" had other plans.

An everlasting love?

Ah yes, relationships. We just love having them, do we not? You meet that special person, and you are instantly swept up in the love that you have for each other. You think that they will support you through it all, and that it was fate that you had met one another. What some people fail to realize is that sometimes relationships have challenging moments, and those challenging moments require patience and understanding. During my undergraduate and graduate years, I had dated a few men who I thought would be present for me even during my darkest moments. I remember dating this one young man throughout my sophomore year of college. This man was one of those people who was only there for me when everything was going well. He was not one to stand by my side when life became difficult.

The night before, my first surgery, I had called and told my partner at the time about my retinal detachment. I explained that I needed to undergo emergency surgery to reattach my retina. He had a bunch of his friends over his house that night, and they were playing video games. While we were on the phone, he did not seem concerned about me or my situation. He did not offer to come with me to my surgery the next day nor did he attempt to see me the night before. I desperately wanted him to care. Eventually, after a few days of recovery, he came to see me after my first procedure. When I saw him, I had a plastic shield covering my right eye and it was packed with gauze to stop my eye from weeping. As I was sitting at the dining room table eating dinner with my parents and partner, he informed us in passing that he was fine with being alone, and that he did not need to be in a relationship. I was so delirious from the pain medication that I was taking, so I barely had time to even register what he had said to me. Honestly, that statement should have been a clue that he was not invested in the relationship.

Another time, this same partner and I had gone out to dinner. As we were eating, he took a long look at me, and he said, "I cannot wait for you to get better so that you can start doing things again." Once again, I had no idea how to respond. I thought to myself: Are you serious? Do you not see what I am going through? Do you not understand that I am trying to put the pieces of my life back together? Eventually, our relationship ended, and unfortunately, during the fall semester, I was stuck taking a class with him and his best friend after we had broken up. He ignored me in that class for quite a while. Do you want to know when he started talking to me again? Well, at the time, I was wearing glasses because I could not wear my contacts yet. I had these square, black-framed glasses with thick lenses because of my nearsightedness. To be honest, I felt ugly while wearing those glasses, and my self-esteem was at an all-time low. Once I was able to wear my contact lenses, and I started to look like my old self again, he finally paid attention to me. Now that I think about it, I need to ask you this question: Are we really that vain? Is physical appearance that important? In my opinion, I would like to think that what is inside of a person's soul is what truly matters. Physical characteristics fade over time, but your heart never changes. Regrettably, he did not feel the same way.

My partner during graduate school had zero understanding of my limitations. Because of my surgeries and my condition, I am unable to go on rollercoasters or any rides that have substantial g-force. One day, he kept asking my mom regarding my restrictions, "What did the doctor really say?" As my mom grew increasingly upset at my partner's lack of understanding and overall attitude, she explained the fact that I am limited to the rides that I am able to go on. As he asked the same question over and over again, he could not come to terms with the fact that his girlfriend was impaired. Eventually, it sunk in, and his jaw dropped. Clearly, this was not the answer that he had wanted to hear. He wanted a girlfriend who could keep up with him. He did not want someone who could potentially be a millstone around his neck. Ultimately, I began to feel like I was this huge cross to bear, and I was nothing but a nuisance to other people.

On a separate note, please understand that whenever I start talking to a potential romantic partner, I am always upfront about my condition. I feel that it is important that I am honest with them about what I can and cannot do. The responses that I receive from possible partners are varied. Some people genuinely understand my limitations, and their kindness is truly a refreshing experience. Others may understand at first, but as time goes on, and reality sets in, they become frustrated with the given circumstances. Unfortunately, there have been moments when I was getting to know someone, and I was upfront with them about my visual impairment. The next day, I never heard from them again.

Nice to see you, too

Even acquaintances of mine would have something to say about my eye or my appearance as a whole. One day, I was going to the supermarket with my mom. This outing was one of the first times that I had left my home in weeks since my first surgery. I was feeling very depressed and angry about my circumstances. I was also dreading going into the store that day. Despite these feelings, I got out of the car and walked into the supermarket. My mom and I knew a woman who worked behind the deli counter. My mom said hello to her, and she had asked the woman how she was doing. The woman replied that she was doing well, and she had proceeded to ask my mom the same question. My mom replied, "Stephanie just had eye surgery for a detached retina." At that point in time, my eye was red, and because of the surgery, my pupil was significantly enlarged. So, imagine seeing someone whose left eye pupil is normal sized, and her right eye pupil is so large that you can barely see her iris. That was the look that

I was working with that day. Anyway, in response to my mom's statement, the woman took one look at me and said, "That looks horrible." It took every ounce of my being to not cry on the spot. At that moment, I felt like I was suffocating. I was humiliated, and I wished that the floor would swallow me whole. Needless to say, my mom and I finished our shopping, and when I got into the car, I started to cry. I remember feeling so helpless and small. My mom looked at me and said, "Steph, she just doesn't understand." Through my tears, I turned to my mom and said to her, "Mom, people need to start having a basic understanding of these things."

Dinner and a show

While in public, another acquaintance of mine seemed to have taken joy in pointing out my "flaws." One evening, my family and I went out to dinner. We knew the owners of the restaurant, and we enjoyed speaking with them. That night, while we were eating dinner, my parents proceeded to tell the owners about my first retinal detachment. I still was wearing black-framed glasses because it had not been long after my surgery had taken place. One of the owners teased me about my glasses and how goofy they looked. At first, I tried to laugh it off. However, the owner kept teasing me about my glasses, and I began to feel uncomfortable. I found his banter at my expense to be annoying, and quite frankly, his behavior was inappropriate. Here again, we have a blatant disregard for people's feelings and a complete misunderstanding of experiences pertaining to disability. Needless to say, as the teasing ensured, my mom took one look at the owner, and she said to him, "That is enough."

She can't even go on rides

Now, this event that took place is one of my favorite examples of ableism and stigma. I was hesitant to put this example into my book; however, you and I have an agreement that I would be honest with you and tell you the truth about my experiences. This one particular occurrence happened after my 23rd birthday trip to Walt Disney World in Orlando, Florida during June 2015. I was dating a young man who was extremely understanding of my disability, and he showed me compassion when I needed it the most. His brother was dating another young woman, and I think that there was some friction between us due to external circumstances. One day, after I had returned from my vacation, this woman had made a comment on Twitter about the pictures that I had uploaded from my trip on Facebook. She remarked at the poor quality of my photos, and how terrible they looked. Her friend had agreed with the less than idea quality of the photos, and, in response to her friend, she had written the following statement: "Dude, they didn't meet one single character, and she can't even go on rides." In the end, when I had explained to her the details surrounding my condition, the woman apologized for her behavior towards me, and since then, we have become good acquaintances. I have long ago forgiven her for what she had said, but at the time, it still hurt me to the core. Prior to my surgeries, I loved going on rides. In my mind, the bigger the ride the better it was. After both retinal detachments, my retina specialist informed me that my choice rides were the merry-go-round and *It's a Small World*.

Stay hidden at all costs

Due to the onslaught of stigma and ableist comments that I had experienced, I did everything that I could to conceal the fact that I had a disability. I thought that because my disability was invisible, people would not suspect that there was anything "wrong" with me. At the time, my goal was to draw as little attention as possible to myself. I fixated on fitting in, and I wanted people to see me the same way prior to my disability. So, I avoided discussing my visual impairment, and I tried to look as "normal" as possible. My thought process was: If my impairment is out of sight, then my impairment is out of mind. Truthfully, my visual impairment was never out of sight nor was it ever out of my mind. In fact, I spent so much time focusing on my disability that I had forgotten how to enjoy life. There was this constant need within me to look and feel "perfect." I will admit that the need to hide my disability made me vain for a short period of time. This need translated into me always checking myself in the mirror and making sure that I was deemed suitable for society. It is no secret that my experiences with retinal detachment warped how I perceived myself; however, I will be covering this topic further in Chapter 7.

Disability stigma: Breaking the cycle

As I have mentioned before, disability stigma and ableism are pervasive. Biases, assumptions, and perceptions pertaining to disability stoke the fires of hatred, isolation, and concealment that, unfortunately, are often directed toward this community. I implore you to understand that your words and actions carry significant consequences. It is like casting a stone into a lake. As soon as that stone hits the water, a ripple effect occurs. Please keep this in mind as you speak to those with visual impairments and other forms of disability. Just like you, we have feelings, and we deserve to be treated with the same respect and dignity. Let my experiences of disability stigma and ableism be a lesson to you to think before you speak and act. Remember, words hurt, and actions matter. Our next chapter, Chapter 5, will explore the myriad of barriers that visually impaired higher education students endure while on their college and university campuses.

5
Barriers to inclusivity

Before we officially begin this chapter, I think that we need to take some time to define the term *barrier*. First, I will provide basic definitions of this term. Next, I will define the word *barrier* from a disability standpoint. Then, I will revisit the medical and social models of disability. I briefly introduced you to both of these concepts in Chapter 1; however, I want to provide you with a deeper understanding of them. I believe the barriers that visually impaired higher education students experience are connected to both models of disability. For this reason, we need to expand our knowledge of these frameworks. Finally, we will narrow our focus, and we will explore the different types of barriers that visually impaired higher education students face while obtaining their college degrees.

What is a barrier?

In simple terms, the word *barrier* is defined as any kind of boundary or limit (Dictionary.com, 2024). There is an additional definition of this term that I think is quite fitting for this book. *Barriers* can also be described as something that restricts or hinders access, progress, etc. (Dictionary.com, 2024). There is one particular word that I want you to keep in mind when reviewing the second definition. That word is *access*. The reason that I want you to remember the term *access* is because it will show up again in our discussion of the medical and social models of disability. In addition, I would like you to think about the following questions: What is access? Why is access so important within the context of disability? Are we already not providing accessible environments and resources for people with disabilities?

Now that you have a simplistic understanding of the word *barrier,* and you have started to think about what the term *access* truly means, I want to switch it up a bit. In this next section, we are going to discuss what constitutes a barrier from a disability standpoint.

Barriers pertaining to disability

Generally speaking, individuals with disabilities face numerous barriers which significantly impact their lives (CDC, 2024). Barriers are not just physical in nature. Rather, barriers pertain to elements within a person's life, through their existence or nonexistence, that cause disability and reduce their everyday operation. These factors include the following:

- A shortage of "assistive technology"
- A non-accessible, physical setting
- "Negative attitudes" pertaining to individuals with disabilities
- Policies, services, and systems that either do not exist, or hamper the participation of individuals with disabilities in all walks of life (World Health Organization, 2001, p. 214, cited in CDC, 2024b, p. 1).

Please understand that the barriers associated with disability are extensive, and we have only begun to scratch the surface of this topic. Also, keep in mind that we will revisit disability barriers again within subsequent sections of this chapter. Now, let us explore the medical and social models of disability in detail.

Medical model of disability

The medical model of disability has been around for quite some time. In fact, this paradigm has acted as the dominant model of civilization since the nineteenth century (Mackleprang and Salsgiver, 2009; Peterson and Aguiar 2004; Williams 2001, cited in Zaks, 2024). The name of this model was invented by Dr. Szasz during the middle of the 1950s. The purpose of this devised paradigm was to criticize the practice within psychiatry of identifying mental health problems as illnesses and providing medicinal treatment for these new ailments (Hogan, 2019, cited in Zaks, 2024).

Individuals with mental health problems have long been viewed as atypical, and Dr. Szasz openly criticized psychiatrists for "pathologizing" ordinary behaviors and emotions (Lemert, 1951; Parsons, 1951, cited in Zaks, 2024, p. 3). Szasz also alleged that psychiatrists were concocting mental health diseases for the purposes of implementing order within society (Szasz, 1956; 1960, cited in Zaks, 2024). Ultimately, Szasz believed that there were individuals who endured issues of living; however, he stood by the belief that providing medicine to those with mental health conditions did not assist in stopping the cycles of prejudice, stigma, and poverty. He further ascertained that medicine did not promote changes regarding societal circumstances, expectations pertaining to relationships, and social attitudes. These three components were essential for patients with mental health issues to successfully participate within the public (Albee, 1977; Goffman, 1961; Szasz, 1960, p. 114, cited in Zaks, 2024).

Dr. Szasz was criticized for voicing his opinions pertaining to this model of disability within the realm of psychiatry (Weinstein, 1994, cited in Zaks, 2024). However, within the 1970s, the medical model was the common language that was used to classify conditions of the human body and brain (Begelman, 1971; Hogan, 2019; Williams, 2001, cited in Zaks, 2024).

Basic premise of the medical model

The medical model affirms that disability is a characteristic problem in the person. This paradigm attempts to stabilize or treat the impairment of the individual (Barker, 1948; Barker, Wright, and Gonick, 1946; Dunn, 2011; Fenderson, 1984; Gill, Kewman, and Brannon, 2003; Olkin, Pledger, and Anderson, 2003; Wright, 1960; 1983, cited in Rosa et al., 2016). Additionally, the medical model of disability establishes the "ableist" notion that only acknowledges people who are characteristically in good health and who are regarded as having standard levels of ability and bodily fitness. An example of this idea would be using two legs to walk in a normal manner (Friedman and Owen, 2017; cited in Ma and Mak, 2024, p. 3).

There is a general agreement within academia that since the nineteenth century, one central purpose of the medical model of disability was to classify individuals as abnormal or normal. If an individual was deemed abnormal, they would be refused access to communal resources, their life prospects would be limited, and their activities and power would be taken away (Barton, 2018; Baynton, 2013; Drake, 2018; Riddell, 2018, cited in Zaks, 2024).

Social model of disability

In 1975, associates of the "Union of the Physically Impaired Against Segregation" wrote a paper that openly criticized the public for being the cause of disability. The members of this group that was based in London stated that society was responsible for creating barriers that limited the participation levels for individuals with disabilities (UPIAS, 1976, cited in Zaks, 2024, p. 6). Five years later, during the 1980s, the social model of disability was espoused by a British sociology instructor named Michael Oliver (Oliver, 1990, cited in Hogan, 2019; Zaks, 2024). Oliver himself had a disability, and he expressed that an individual's incapacity to do something was due to societal conditions (Oliver, 1983, cited in Zaks, 2024).

Basic premise of the social model

The social model sustains the belief that disability is not a personified flaw. Instead, disability is a notion that is contrived by history and the community (Barnes, 1990; Oliver, 1990; Shakespeare, 2013, cited in Zaks, 2024). In basic terms, as stated within the aforementioned paragraph, societal characteristics can fabricate an individual's inability to do something. From a historical standpoint, events that have occurred within a history's timeline can create brains and bodies that are considered disabled (Zaks,

2024). Additionally, within this model, disability is viewed as one component of an individual's identity. Viewing disability in this manner is similar to how one views other aspects of a person's identity such as ethnicity, gender, or race (Olkin, 2022). Essentially, the social model ascertains that if disability is constructed on the basis of societal events, expectations, and conditions, then it certainly can be dismantled (Wendell, 1989, cited in, Zaks, 2024).

Disability culture

Throughout the disability movement, individuals with disabilities communicated their experiences and perceptions through art, and they demonstrated "pride in their unique bodies and brains" (Brown, 2003; Invitation to Dance, 2014; Sutherland, 1989, cited in Zaks, 2024, p. 8.). This statement leads us to another concept that I would like to briefly discuss. This concept is called disability culture. During the 1960s, the disability rights movement began to take shape. In the 1970s, there was a substantial increase in the number of disability communities. This increase resulted in the disability culture movement (Peters, 2024). So, you might be asking yourselves: What is disability culture? Well, disability culture is defined as the viewpoints, expressions, and artifacts that were created by individuals with disabilities. The purpose of these creations is for individuals with disabilities to portray their lived experiences (Brown, 2002). In essence, disability provides people within this community with feelings of belonging (UMass, 2024).

Disability Rag

One of the many artifacts pertaining to disability was the magazine titled *The Disability Rag*. Also known as *The Rag and Ragged*

Edge, this periodical was originally started by Mary Johnson. Johnson served as editor of this magazine (Ervin, 2009). With the Advocado Press acting as publisher starting in 1981, *The Disability Rag* was a revolutionary piece of journalism.

For over a 25-year period, this magazine printed a variety of editorials and opinion articles that were authored by people with disabilities. In essence, *The Disability Rag,* pictured in Figure 16 was regarded as one of the most poignant disability rights movement publications (Center for Accessible Living, n.d.; The Advocado Press, 1983).

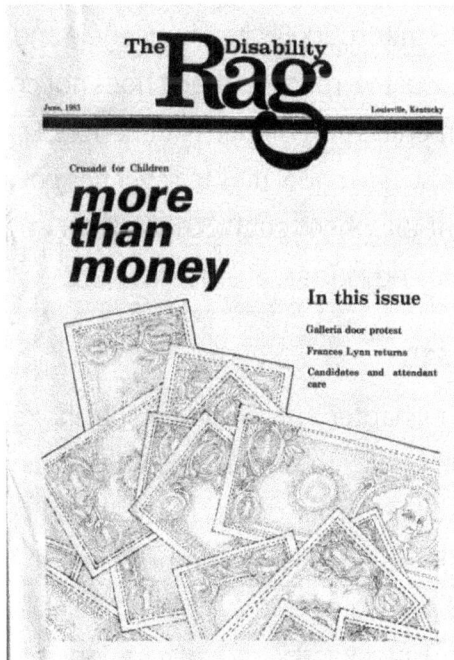

Figure 16. The Disability Rag

Courtesy of the Advocado Press (1983).

Criticisms of the social model of disability

Although the social model of disability has paved the way for disability rights activism and has promoted an improved understanding of disability as a whole, this paradigm is not free from criticism. One critique of the social model is that it does not consider differences among people with disabilities. In other words, it has been implied that this model overlooks how different forms of oppression such as racism and sexism intersect. Contextually speaking, the idea of intersectionality is that ableism is not separate from other oppressed identities (Fitzgerald, 2006; Flintoff, Fitzgerald, and Scraton, 2008, cited in Haegele and Hodge, 2016). Another critique of this model is that it does not consider an individual's impairment as part of their experiences. Essentially, critics believe that the social model tries to sever ties between disability and impairment (Bingham et al., 2013; Palmer and Harley, 2012, cited in Haegele and Hodge, 2016).

Bias persists

As indicated in Chapter 1, there were specific regulations that compelled the public to supply accommodations to individuals with disabilities. This demand for accommodations was characteristic of the disability movement, and it was one of the many activities pertaining to the social model (Oliver, 2004, cited in Zaks, 2024). However, biased perceptions and standpoints toward individuals with disabilities persevered. There was the ever-present belief that people with disabilities were a burden to society, and they were undeserving of opportunity and access (Zaks, 2024).

Now that we have defined the term *barrier* from a basic and disability standpoint, and we have learned about the medical and social models of disability, it is time to continue with our journey. In this next section, we will explore the specific barriers that higher education students with visual impairments endure during their studies.

Barriers for visually impaired students

There are multiple barriers that visually impaired higher education students face while enrolled in their college or university of choice. Let us proceed with learning about these roadblocks!

Issues with admissions

Admissions and programs of recruitment can act as the initial barrier that students with visual impairments experience within higher education. There is a lack of knowledge concerning the accommodations that are accessible to these students. Often, the materials that are presented by the recruiter are not accessibly formatted (Reed and Curtis, 2012, cited in Ostrowski, 2016).

Issues with accommodations

Numerous students who are visually impaired need additional time to finish the programs of education that they are enrolled in. A problem that pertains to accommodations is retention. The literature states that keeping these students enrolled within higher education institutions is a constant worry (Getzel, 2008). Generally speaking, students who are newly registered within their colleges or universities go through an adjustment period as they familiarize themselves with their new environment. However, students who have disabilities need to become familiar with the accommodation process (Ostrowski, 2016). Recall in Chapters 1 and 2 that students must self-identify as having a disability (Aquino and Bittinger, 2019). The reality is if the student does not self-advocate for themselves, then they are not going to obtain the necessary accommodations that are essential for their success. The problem with the accommodation process is that it can be a daunting procedure, and there is a lack of knowledge pertaining to this process (Getzel, 2008; Scott, McGuire, and Shaw, 2003, cited in Ostrowski, 2016).

Issues with technology access

One of the most enduring challenges for students with visual impairments is appropriate access to support (Ostrowski, 2016). Assistive technology as well as information and communication technologies have streamlined access for visually impaired individuals on the basis of communication, socialization, mobility, and education (Al-Jarf, 2021, cited in Kija and Mgumba, 2024). Some of the devices and software that are available for this community include:

- Software that translates Braille
- Software that magnifies words
- Systems that provide "voice over internet protocol (VoIP)"
- Screen readers and scanners
- Digital textbooks that talk
- "Refreshable Braille displays"
- "Audio-tactile maps" of college and university campuses (Al-Jarf, 2021; Goodley, Lawthom, and Liddiard, 2021; Kapperman, Kelly, and Koster, 2018, cited in Kija and Mgumba, 2024, p. 3)
- Transportable notetakers (Sparabary, Kelley, and Romack, 2021).

Even though assistive technology is available, research shows that students who are visually impaired have issues with using and accessing these devices. Some of these issues include a shortage of specialists who are well-versed in assistive technology, unpredictable policies, a disinterest in assistive technology usage, and unsuitable universal design (Kamaghe, Luhanga, and Kisangiri, 2020; Kisanga and Kisanga, 2020; Opie, 2018; Pavithran, 2017; Wu, 2018, cited in Kija and Mgumba, 2024).

On a separate note, for those of you who are wondering what the phrase *universal design for learning* is, you have come to the right place! Simplistically speaking, *universal design for learning* is defined as an approach to teaching that attempts to accommodate the capabilities and requests of all student learners. This method of teaching works to remove pointless barriers within the process of learning. Under this pedagogy, students participate in the learning process in multiple ways, and students are supplied with choices when displaying their learning of course material. Faculty creates a learning environment that is grounded in flexibility. Alternatively speaking, information is supplied to the student in many different ways (Cornell University, 2024).

Issues with expensive technology

Assistive technology for students with visual impairments can be quite expensive (Kija and Mgumba, 2024; Ostrowski, 2016). These students face massive amounts of reading requirements, and textbooks often contain illustrations such as equations and pictures that are occasionally available in additional formats. Furthermore, converting textbooks into braille can be pricey (D'Andrea, 2012, cited in Ostrowski, 2016).

Issues with the campus environment

Research has shown that students with visual impairments can experience unfamiliarity within their college or university campuses. Lourens and Swartz (2016) conducted a study where they interviewed 15 higher-education students with visual impairments. Within this study, the authors asked participants about their lived experiences while on their university campus. They also examined how their participants' disability was experienced within the context of their bodies and the campus environment. It was discovered that the participants felt that they were not considered when their university campus was designed. For example, there were some students within the study who visited their campus early, and they paid money for an orientation and mobility teacher. The purpose of this instructor was to educate the participants on their class routes. However, although they felt somewhat prepared after this process, they believed that these preparations were not sufficient for the everyday task of walking on-campus (Lourens and Swartz, 2016). In addition to these challenges, it was discovered that some of the students felt that the on-campus environment could possibly be unsafe (Lourens and Swartz, 2016).

Issues with socialization

Lourens and Swartz (2016) also found that some of the participants within their study did not feel a sense of belonging among their fellow students. Additionally, participants who only had partial vision stated that they had to work hard to be accepted by other pupils. Frequently, the participants' had what is called an invisible disability. As a result of this classification, their disabilities were challenging to identify, and participants were misunderstood when socially interacting with others (Lourens and Swartz, 2016).

Engagement, community, belonging, access, and disability

This last barrier is one that can be applied to all disabilities. Prior to and currently doing research for this book, I have found that community, belonging, access, and engagement initiatives within higher education are lacking when it comes to disability. This is an alarming discovery considering that there has been an increase in the number of students with disabilities attending higher education institutions (U.S. Department of Education, 2016, cited in Scheef, Caniglia, and Barrio, 2020). Let us stop and think for a second: If colleges and universities are supposed to promote community, belonging, access, and engagement for all students attending their institutions, then why are we not talking about disability? Why is rhetoric pertaining to disability lacking?

Conclusion

Wow! We have covered so much ground in this chapter! Let us take a moment to reflect on how much we have learned! We have learned about what constitutes a barrier, what a barrier is pertaining to disability, the medical and social models of disability, and the various barriers that visually impaired higher education students experience on their campuses! You even learned about disability culture and *The Disability Rag*. How amazing is that! Now, please understand that this chapter was more from a practical and impersonal standpoint. This next chapter, Chapter 6, is going to take a different direction. As I had said in my introduction, Chapter 6 is where my story becomes a bit dark. In this space, we are going to talk about mental health and visual impairments. While I will provide you with some literature regarding this concept, my plan is to share my own mental health experiences with you. A word of caution: Chapter 6 will introduce you to some heavy topics such as post-traumatic stress disorder, depression, anxiety, and suicidal ideation. However, it is time that everyone knew the truth regarding my experiences.

6
PTSD, anxiety, and depression, oh my!

"Look at you, you're disgusting. Who would ever want to be with you?"

"You know that your kids are going to have this condition, right?"

"You're a defective model of a human being."

"The world would be better off without you in it."

"Don't even try to have kids. Your defective genes are going to ruin their lives."

"You are so ugly."

"You bring no purpose to this world. All you do is make people's lives miserable."

"You're such a burden."

"You can't do anything right."

"No one will ever love you."

"Kill yourself. Just end it now."

"I just don't want to live anymore."

Those aforementioned statements, which are horrible and ugly, are just some of the many thoughts that plagued me on a daily basis while I was recovering from my eye surgeries and the subsequent years that followed after my surgeries occurred. My surgeries left me as a shell of a human being, and I felt like there was no end to the pain that I was experiencing. As I look back on that dark period of my life, I realize that I was deeply traumatized. My perceptions of myself were completely warped, and I did not know how to move forward. I used to think that trauma was such a foreign concept when it pertained to higher education students. Granted, I was only 20 and 22 years old, so the idea that I was suffering from mental health issues such as post-traumatic stress disorder, depression, suicidal ideation, and anxiety was unfathomable. However, trauma is more common among college and university students than one realizes. Like a disease, trauma can affect anyone at any age at any time. This idea is a painful reality that we must live with. Ultimately, the key message that we must all remember is the following: In a split second, our life paths can instantly change.

What is trauma?

Trauma is defined as the experiences in which a person's internal capabilities are inadequate to handle stressors from the external environment (Hoch et al., 2015, cited in Davidson, n.d.). Some people who have experienced trauma present symptoms of stress during the initial few weeks; however, they revert back to their typical levels of emotional and physical health (Felitti et al., 1998, cited in Davidson, n.d.). This was pretty much the case for me after my first eye surgery. While the first surgery was traumatic, and I felt as though life had knocked me down, I was able to get back up on my feet. As I had said in previous chapters, I had this fixation where I was concerned that my friends and classmates were moving ahead of me in their studies and in their lives. My initial recovery was fueled by the motivation to show others that this blip in the radar system did not affect me, and I was still on track to be the model student with a 3.94 GPA.

However, my second surgery compounded my initial trauma. Like my first surgery, I attempted to start out strong and to show other people that I was okay. Unfortunately, my attempts failed. Essentially, there was a buildup of unresolved trauma that resulted in mental health issues that still continue to impact my life today. Even individuals who do not display instantaneous or severe symptoms of trauma might endure some amount of emotional stress that intensifies or continues over a period of time (Felitti et al., 1998, cited in Davidson, n.d.).

Trauma-related statistics

I took the liberty of providing you with some statistics regarding trauma within the United States. I would also like to highlight important statistical information pertaining to vision loss and mental health from the Center for Disease Control and Prevention (CDC). Below are a few key facts to consider as you are reading this chapter:

- Higher education students are susceptible to enduring a new, possibly traumatic event
- As much as 50 percent of higher education students are subjected to a new, possibly traumatic event during the first year of their college experience (Galatzer-Levy et al., 2012, cited in Davidson, n.d., p. 5).
- Trauma increases the likelihood of experiencing depression
- There is a higher probability that symptoms of trauma and depression will occur at the same time (Kilpatrick et al., 2003;

O'Donnell, Creamer, and Pattison, 2004; Rytwinski et al., 2013, cited in Davidson, n.d., p. 5).

- Loss of vision has been correlated to feelings of fear, anxiety, and apprehension, communal isolation, and lonesomeness
- Depression commonly occurs among people who have experienced loss of their vision
- According to a study that was conducted by the CDC, young adults who have experienced vision loss had an approximately five times higher risk of developing severe depression or anxiety in comparison to adults who are older in age
- This same study conducted by the CDC also found that one in four adults who experienced loss of their vision stated that they had depression or anxiety (CDC, 2024a, p. 1).

Now that we have established what the term *trauma* means, and we have discussed some relevant statistics regarding trauma and vision loss, we shall go back in time to the moments when I experienced Post Traumatic Stress Disorder (PTSD), depression, suicidal ideation, and anxiety as a visually impaired woman. I will also provide you with a basic understanding of these terms, and I will talk about how these mental health disorders impact those who are affected by visual impairment.

What is post-traumatic stress disorder?

PTSD is a condition that is acquired in some individuals when they experience a scary, traumatizing, or alarming event. PTSD can occur at any age, and those who have been inflicted by this disorder might experience feelings of fright or stress even when they are free from danger. Symptoms of post-traumatic stress disorder typically happen within three months after the traumatizing event has occurred; however, these symptoms can occur after three months. In order to receive a diagnosis of PTSD, a grown adult must experience symptoms over a one-month period, and symptoms must interfere with everyday aspects of an individual's life. Additionally, symptoms cannot be related to abuse of substances, additional illnesses, or medication (National Institute of Mental Health, 2024).

Additionally, to receive a diagnosis of PTSD, an adult must have specific symptoms for no less than a one-month period. Each of these symptoms falls under four important categories. These categories include symptoms of re-experiencing, symptoms of avoidance, symptoms of reactivity and arousal, and symptoms pertaining to cognition and mood. Within these categories, a person must experience no less than one symptom of re-experiencing, no less than one symptom of avoidance, at a minimum of two symptoms of reactivity and arousal, and at a minimum of two symptoms pertaining to cognition and mood (National Institute of Mental Health, 2024). In the subsequent sections, I will highlight the symptoms that I experienced after both eye surgeries. Please keep in mind that PTSD is more predominant among people with visual impairments than those who are a part of mainstream society (Bonsaksen, Brunes, and Heir, 2022).

Symptoms of re-experience

My PTSD symptoms started to officially occur within six months after my second surgery. Granted, while recovering from my first surgery, I would say that I had some symptoms of PTSD; however, they were much more severe after my second surgery.

Collectively, during my first and second eye surgeries, I experienced the following symptoms:

- Enduring physical symptoms of stress
- Dreaming or having frequent memories pertaining to my eye surgeries
- Enduring flashbacks of my surgeries which would result in physical symptoms such as my heart racing
- Experiencing disturbing thoughts (National Institute of Mental Health, 2024).

While I was recovering from my surgeries, I never truly felt safe. Every single day, I lived in fear of my retina detaching again. Tension took on a permanent residence within my body. As the days went by, and I held my muscles tight, I would pray to God that I would make it through another day detachment-free. When evening came, and I could, for a fleeting moment, escape the trauma that enveloped me, the muscles within my body would begin to relax. Upon relaxing my muscles, I would begin to feel flu-like symptoms from the relentless stress that I felt throughout the day.

Sometimes, during the day, or before I went to sleep, I would experience flashbacks and memories of my eye surgeries. As I would lay in bed, or sit on the couch, I remembered everything. I remembered my first surgery where I was lying on the hospital bed waiting to be wheeled down to the operating room. I remembered finally being transported to the operating room and listening to the kind nurses calmly reassuring me that I would be okay. I would picture me being wheeled away from my parents who were my source of safety and strength. Finally,

I would see my anesthesiologist standing over top of me, and saying to me, "Okay, Stephanie, you're going to go to sleep now." Within a split second, I was under the effects of the anesthesia, and everything went black. I was gone from the world for just a little while.

When you are a survivor of retinal detachment, and yes, I consider myself to be a survivor, you vividly remember the many times that you had to go back to your retinal specialist for follow-up appointments. After your first post-op appointment after surgery, you see your retina specialist one week later. Once your one-week appointment has passed and there are no further issues with your vision, your next retina appointment is scheduled for two weeks, then four weeks, then one month later, and so on. When you finally reach the one-year appointment milestone, it is truly a cause for celebration. You look back on how far you have come, and you think to yourself, "Yes, I finally beat this!" However, while you reminisce on your journey, you are plagued with the memories of lying down on the examination chair and being told by your retina specialist to look up, look down, look to the right, and look to the left as they complete your retina examination. You remember the stinging sensation of the dilation drops going into your eyes and the harsh lights that were used to complete the examination. You remember thinking to yourself, "Please, let me get through this." As I remembered all of these moments, my heart would begin to pound out of its chest cavity. My breathing would quicken, and I would start to cry. At the time, having to remember moments like this was horrifying, and I felt like they were constantly haunting me. The only time that I could escape the pain was through sleep. However, upon waking up the next morning, the darkness would be there, waiting to greet me like an old friend.

Symptoms of avoidance

I would often avoid places and events that would remind me of my trauma (National Institute of Mental Health, 2024). For me, just walking out of my home could send me into a downward spiral of trauma-induced panic. All stores and restaurants were deemed unsafe to me. I could not even go to a supermarket for fear that my retina would detach again. All I had wanted to do was to stay home and be within the confines of my bedroom. It was only within my home that I truly felt safe. The rest of the world was like a ticking time bomb.

Even as I write this section, I cannot help but feel sad that my level of fear had truly gotten to this point. I was once a vivacious young woman who loved to go out with her friends, family, and partners. I was always on the move, and the fact that I had gone from going out all of the time to not even wanting to leave my home to run an errand is unbelievable to me. Even today, after eleven years of being detachment free, sometimes that old panic creeps in, and I begin to feel that same fear that I had felt all those years ago.

In addition to avoiding events or places that served as reminders of my trauma, I actively avoided feelings or thoughts that pertained to my eye surgeries (National Institute of Mental Health, 2024). Later, during my recovery process, I would tell myself, "Listen, you need to start facing and accepting what had happened to you." As I tried to remember the series of events that took place during my surgeries, I became extremely upset. My mind would scream, "Stop!" over and over again. I realized that I was not ready to face my demons, and I had no choice but to give in and let my mind rest.

After I had undergone my vitrectomy, which was my second surgery, I had to lay on my left side for five days so that the gas bubble would flatten the retina at the correct angle. Even when I was sitting up, I had to keep my head tilted to the side. To this day, I cannot really lay on my left side or tilt my head in that direction because it brings back so many painful memories for me. This small action unleashes flashbacks of neck aches, sadness, and heartache.

Symptoms of reactivity and arousal

There are six sub-symptoms that fall under this category. Out of the six characteristics, I had four. These sub-symptoms include:

- Feeling like you are on edge, feeling tense, and being on guard
- You are easily startled
- You feel irritable, you exhibit aggressive behavior, and you demonstrate anger
- You engage in destructive, uncertain, or irresponsible behavior (National Institute of Mental Health, 2024).

Ironically, these symptoms occur on a constant basis. There is no rest from these painful feelings. What is even worse is the fact that these feelings bleed into other areas of your life. You might have issues with eating, concentrating, or sleeping (National

Institute of Mental Health, 2024). I was so angry about what had happened to me. I felt no love towards the world. Day after day, I would sit on the couch, and I would think to myself, "Why did this have to happen to me? What did I do to deserve this? Why couldn't my body just behave normally?" My mother was the target of my outbursts. She did everything that she could to make sure that I was taken care of; however, all I did was scream at her because of my circumstances. To this day, I look back on my behavior with so much shame and regret. My mother did not deserve this type of treatment from me. She was only trying to help me through a difficult time.

My anger was not just directed at my mother. I was prone to aggressive outbursts that were directed towards my father and my partner at the time. I would scream, yell, and say condescending things that delivered a slow burn. Again, all that they tried to do was help me; however, all I could see was red. Ultimately, I was angry at everyone and everything. I would look at my social media newsfeeds, and I would see everyone who I knew living their best lives. Back then, I was so impressionable, and I took everything that I saw at face value. I truly believed that they had everything, and I had nothing. While the rest of the world kept turning, I was left behind to rot away.

I was also always on edge. I felt like something big and bad was about to happen to me. I lived my life in fear. Whenever someone tried to get my attention, I would jump and say "What? What's the matter?" Whenever I reacted in this manner, I would be met with looks of confusion from other people. Whenever I would go out to restaurants and people would be talking at the table,

I would zone out. I would get this blank look on my face, and I would not hear a word that they were saying. When someone would ask me a question, I would be forced to go back into reality, and I would answer the question to the best of my abilities. Physically, during that time, my stomach would be in knots, and my chest would feel heavy.

My surgeries also had an impact on my decision-making skills. Prior to my surgeries and to my disability, I always took pride in the fact that I could make good decisions for myself. After my surgeries, my choices became wayward and unclear. I began to surround myself with toxic people who were simply not good for my well-being. I could not determine the next steps of my life, and who I was meant to be in this world. I found myself jumping from one idea to the next when it came to my future. In later years, I endured emotional abuse from subsequent partners, and I tried to tell myself that their behavior was okay when in reality, it was anything but okay. My self-esteem was so low, and I felt that I did not deserve peace and happiness. I would think to myself, "I am a defective model of a human being, so why should I feel that I deserve any better?"

Symptoms of mood and cognition

I experienced six out of the seven sub-symptoms pertaining to mood and cognition. The sub-symptoms that I experienced were the following:

- Thinking negatively about society and myself
- Blaming myself and others
- Experiencing shame, guilt, anger, and fear

- Loss of interest in fun activities
- Feeling socially isolated
- Having a hard time feeling happy or satisfied (National Institute of Mental Health, 2024).

I felt as though the color was drained from the world. The black-and-white void that I had created for myself pervaded my existence. There was no happiness for me. In just a few short months, I had lost part of my vision, I had lost my grandmother to cancer, and I had lost my gramps. I felt as though there was no coming back from all of that trauma. In addition, I had such a low self-perception that I barely recognized myself in the mirror. I saw who I had become, and I did not like the image that was reflected back at me. I felt ugly in more ways than one both physically and mentally. I felt such shame for my disability, and I felt like this was all my fault, that I had somehow caused all of this to happen.

My surgeries and disability made me feel like a walking freak. At my grandmother's funeral, I had to wear a green bracelet which alerted others that I had a gas bubble in my eye. I had to wear this bracelet until my gas bubble dissipated (Zheutlin, Garber, and Glazer, n.d.). I hated wearing that green bracelet. It basically screamed, "Hey! I have a problem!" In my mind, this scenario would play out in my head like I was trapped within a cage at a carnival freakshow. The ringleader of the show would say, "Step right up and witness the girl with the gas bubble in her eye! Only 50 cents to see the freak with defective eyes!" I was so ashamed of who I had become. I did not feel beautiful, and I did not feel like a survivor. In my heart, I knew that I was not living. I was merely existing.

What is anxiety?

In addition to PTSD, I also suffered from anxiety. Worldwide, conditions pertaining to anxiety are the most commonplace mental ailments. In 2019, 301 million individuals were affected by this type of disorder. Additionally, women are more likely to be impacted by anxiety conditions than men (World Health Organization, 2023a, p. 1). From a visual impairment standpoint, anxiety conditions and anxiety are more frequently experienced by individuals who are visually impaired as compared to those within general society. In fact, approximately 4–6 percent of individuals with visual impairments are inflicted by anxiety conditions, and one-third endure anxiety and/or depression (Binder, Wrzesińska, and Kocur, 2020, p. 279).

Individuals who have an anxiety disorder might endure extreme worry or fear regarding particular circumstances, or they might experience worry regarding daily affairs. Symptoms of anxiety disorders can occur over a prolonged length of time (World Health Organization, 2023a). There are seven symptoms of anxiety which include the following:

- Feelings of restlessness, tension, or irritability
- Feeling nauseous and having stomach pain
- Having difficulty making decisions or concentrating
- Experiencing palpitations of the heart
- Experiencing tremors, sweating, or shaking
- Having a hard time sleeping
- Having feelings of imminent doom, panic, or vulnerability (World Health Organization, 2023a).

My experiences with anxiety

I will admit that I have always been an anxious person; however, the anxiety that I used to feel was manageable and it did not significantly impact on my quality of life. After my surgeries, my anxiety got out of control. Throughout my days, I would feel an ever-present tension that pervaded my chest cavity. My heart would beat and palpitate at increased rates. I found it hard to catch my breath, and my chest ached with every second of the day. My stomach would constantly be in knots because I was terrified that I would need to be rushed back to Wills Eye Hospital for emergency surgery.

Under the direction of my retina specialist, I would check my right eye for any new black veils or floaters within my field of vision. I even had special places in my home where I could diligently make sure that a new detachment had not formed. First, I would stand in my bathroom, I would put my hand over my left eye, and I would look straight ahead in the mirror. I used the lights that hung over my bathroom mirror to determine if my vision loss had grown. There were three lights in a row, and I determined that my primary vision loss only covered one of the overhead lights. Each day, I would do this test. If my vision loss only covered the first light, then I was safe.

The second step in this process was to look out of my backyard door in the sunroom. The reason that I conducted a second check was because I wanted to make sure that I did not miss anything new or strange with my vision. In addition, the lighting was different, so I knew that I would be able to make a correct comparison. As I looked out the sunroom door, I would cover my left eye, and I would conduct the same check. If it was deter-mined that my vision loss had not grown by way of outdoor lighting, then I knew that I was in the clear. Mind you, I did not conduct my checks only once a day. These checks were obses-sively conducted. I could never get enough reassurance. I always needed more.

When I attempted to leave the house, I tested the patience of everyone around me. I would question the vision loss or the pea-sized, circular floaters that I was seeing in my right eye. My left eye also had and still continues to have floaters in its visual field because I am severely nearsighted. This fact made me even more nervous than I already was.

I remember one time, months after my second surgery took place, I went to the nail salon to have a manicure, a pedicure, and an eyebrow waxing. I just wanted to feel human, and I wanted to feel like myself again. After I had gotten my eyebrows waxed, I began to feel a pain in my right eye. As my partner at the time drove me home from my appointment, I was on the phone with my parents hysterically crying over the pain and the panic that had enveloped me. I ran upstairs to the bathroom to take my contacts out and to put my glasses on. My father rushed into the bathroom to make sure that I was okay. Once it was determined that my eye was alright, I broke down in his arms. Large, gasp-ing sobs emanated from my body, and I felt like a small, vulner-able child.

Every day, I prayed to God that I would go through my daily life without experiencing another detachment. I spent every wak-ing moment filled with panic and nervousness. When nighttime came, I would go into my room, and I would close my door. I would think to myself, "You made it through the day. You're safe now." Only then would I begin to calm down.

To this day, my anxiety levels are still not the same. I find myself feeling nervous when speaking to new people or presenting my research at conferences. Sometimes, I feel dizzy in public places, and I have to excuse myself from those who I am talking to so that I may get my bearings. My anxiety is a constant battle. I wish that I could be calm and collected all of the time; however, that is not the case for me.

What is depression?

Depression, also known as clinical depression or major depressive disorder, is defined as a condition that produces unrelenting feelings of unhappiness. This disorder can also cause an individual to lose interest in everyday activities. Depression can significantly impact how an individual thinks, feels emotions, and conducts themselves (Mayo Clinic Staff, 2022b).

Some of the symptoms pertaining to depression include:

- Feeling hopeless, sad, tearful, or empty
- A lack of sleep or too much sleep
- Feeling worthless, blaming oneself, or focusing on past mistakes
- Decreased levels of energy and exhaustion
- Regular or common thoughts pertaining to death, suicide attempts, suicide, or suicidal ideation
- Weight gain or weight loss (Mayo Clinic Staff, 2022b).

My experiences with depression

I will be honest with you. The truth is, during my experiences with retinal detachment, I did not want to live anymore. I did not see a point in continuing in this world. There were multiple times when I would fantasize about ending my life, and in my mind, I felt as though everyone would be better off without me. I thought that all I did was take up space, so I believed that I would never be missed. The two people who stopped me from committing suicide were my parents. I knew that if I had even attempted to do so, they would never recover. It was them who kept me afloat within the sea of darkness. In addition to wanting to die, all I wanted to do was cry. I could not cry because I was on so many eye drops, and crying would have prolonged my recovery. Every waking moment was focused on keeping calm and not bursting into tears. Unfortunately, I was not always successful, and ultimately, I would give into my sadness.

In addition to experiencing suicidal ideation, I spent a lot of my time sleeping because I was on pain medicine. My body felt weak and heavy with exhaustion. During that time, I think that if I could, I would have slept all day every day. The pain medicine was the culprit behind the excessive sleeping; however, as I had said in a previous section of this chapter, sleep was the only time that I did not feel any emotional pain. For a fleeting moment, I was free.

I also lost a decent amount of weight after my second surgery. I became very skinny, and my parents told me that I needed to eat in order to heal. Looking back, my self-image was significantly damaged. I felt physically ugly, and I think that the main reason that I had lost a lot of weight was because it was something that I could control. My eyes had betrayed me, so this was the only way that I could gain back some power. I started to like the way that I looked. I figured that for what I had lacked in my face I could make up with my body.

Conclusion

The biggest thing that I want you to take away from this chapter is that mental health and visual impairments are strongly connected. These conditions and problems pertaining to this community are real, and they can happen to anyone at any given point in time. We are not guaranteed a clean bill of health, so I want you to understand that if you are struggling with any mental health condition, please realize and understand that you are here on this earth for a reason. You are enough, you matter, and you are capable of anything. Do not let anyone tell you otherwise.

Chapter 7 will provide you with a bit more levity. In this chapter, I will discuss the steps that I had taken to reconstruct my newfound identity as a visually impaired woman. In addition, I will introduce you to some incredible people who helped me find myself along the way, and to whom I owe a significant amount of gratitude. Finding support while on a journey such as this is so important, and I want to highlight how I and other people helped me to pick up the pieces.

7
Forging ahead: Reconstructing my identity

Who I was

Once upon a time, I was a strong, independent woman who had big dreams. I grew up in a family who loved cars and drag racing. One of my hopes and dreams was to learn how to drag race and to follow in my father's footsteps. As a teenager, I drove go-carts, motor and electric scooters, dune buggies, and dirt bikes. I had a metropolitan scooter that I lovingly named *Cherry Bomb*. I live on two acres of land, so I used to ride *Cherry Bomb* for hours in my backyard. In fact, the first question that my dad had asked when we purchased the piece of land was the following, "Can you drive go-carts and scooters back here?" With my pink racing helmet on, I used to pretend that I was riding in the streets of Paris or Italy. I would look up at the sky, and I would daydream about who I was going to be in this world. I had inherited my father's passion for everything car-related, and I loved being able to share this interest with him.

In addition to inheriting my dad's passion for fast cars and fast speeds, I acquired my mother's free-spirited nature. My mom and I used to love going to amusement parks with our family and friends, and we would ride the tallest, fastest rollercoasters that we could possibly find. As the coasters jerked and moved at lightning speed, we would scream and laugh like there was no tomorrow. We loved sharing these moments together, and we were always up for a fun time!

High school years

While I was in high school, I was extremely stubborn and, to be honest, quite sassy. I was never afraid to speak my mind. During those earlier years, I was a young woman who just told it like it was. I could be sarcastic at times, and I had a dry sense of humor. At the same time, I would laugh out loud at the jokes that my friends used to make, and sometimes I could be a bit mischievous. I was involved in every extracurricular activity that you could possibly imagine, and I thought deeply about my future. I had a huge heart, and I would do anything for the people who I cared about the most. In my heart, I knew that I wanted to be someone in this world, and I had the confidence to pursue my dreams. I was a happy, smiling young woman who had friends and family who loved me for who I was. Looking back, I realize how I had taken these moments in my life for granted.

College: The calm before the storm

Prior to my eye surgeries, my freshman and sophomore years of college were filled with large amounts of homework, homecoming celebrations, spending time with friends, and just enjoying everything that college had to offer. I was an 18- and 19-year-old business management major, and I loved going to my classes. I would arrive at class early, and I would wait patiently for the professor to come in and start their lecture. When the professor finally arrived at class, and they began to discuss subjects such as supply and demand, theories of motivation, and the aggregate economy, I would diligently write down every single word that they were saying. I loved the feel of the pen in my hand and the smell of new notebook paper.

Prior to the start of the semester, I would drag my mom to Staples, and we would purchase new notebooks and folders for every subject. The notebooks and folders had to be bright and colorful, and everything had to be properly labeled. The same excitement applied to when I would purchase my textbooks for the upcoming semester. I would think to myself, "Wow! I am going to learn so much in this class!" It was no secret that I loved to learn! Back then, I felt as though life was a dream, and I was the director of my life's movie. I had a purpose, and I knew the direction that I wanted my life to take. This direction significantly changed in August 2012.

Who am I?

After my two surgeries, and the few years after these surgeries took place, I often questioned who I was. The truth is, I did not know who I was, nor did I understand why all of this had happened to me. I felt robbed of so many experiences. For the longest time, I could not drive because I kept having to have new procedures done on my eyes. Because of my surgeries, my driving experience was limited. I could not just get into my car and drive to the nearest coffee shop and purchase a coffee of my choice. I had to depend on someone to take me, and that made me feel like I was such a burden.

Physically, I did not look like myself. As I had said in previous chapters, I had to wear my glasses for long periods of time. In addition to having to wear glasses, my face was broken out in acne because of the stress that I had experienced, and I did not feel like the beautiful, vivacious woman I once was. During my graduate school years, I buried myself in my MBA work. I felt like my schoolwork was something that I could control, and I was proud of my hard work and diligence in completing my degree. As I worked on my homework, I would think to myself, "Someday, I am going to be someone. I will be successful, and I will put this mess behind me."

Pressure cooker

After 2015, which was when my second retinal detachment occurred, I had a lot of unresolved trauma. As the years passed by, I was not coming to terms with my experiences, my grand-mother passing away, or my new identity. As I had told you in Chapter 6, I began to surround myself with people who were not good for my well-being. I did not make the best choices for myself, and I felt like I did not deserve better than the life that I was leading. The pain that I carried with me on a consistent basis kept haunting me, and it was only a matter of time until I snapped.

Breakdown

In summer 2019, I finally had a nervous breakdown. I could not conceal the pain that I was carrying any longer, and I knew that I needed help. By that period of time, my life was not going in the direction that I had planned. I felt like I was on this merry-go-round of uncertainty, and I could not get off the ride. The day that my nervous breakdown occurred, my mom and I went to Olive Garden to have lunch. As we sat in the booth, I stared straight ahead, and I could not say anything to her. I felt so numb, and I knew that at that point, I had finally hit rock bottom. I also realized that I could not keep going down the path that I was on. In my heart, I knew that things needed to change; however, I was not equipped with the tools to get myself back on my feet.

Picking up the pieces

I cannot stress enough how important it is to have support systems when you are going through challenging situations. I was blessed to have such a strong group of friends, family, and professionals who supported me while I was on this journey. I want to take this opportunity to introduce you to some incredible people who helped me find my way back to who I once was, and who I am today. I will also tell you the steps that I took to move forward in reclaiming my identity.

My parents

My parents were my strongest supporters and biggest advocates during this time of my life. I always say that if I did not have my parents supporting me, I do not know where I would be today. My mom singlehandedly drove me to every single retina appointment imaginable. During my recovery, she put eye drops in my eyes, and she changed the gauze in my eye patch when my eye was weeping from the surgeries. She would sit at the computer, and she would learn everything that she possibly could about the condition called retinal detachment. She was the woman who told me as I was lying down on the couch after my second surgery, "Steph, you can either sit there and continue to be depressed, or you can get up from the couch, and you can start to accept what has happened to you." My mom also suggested that I start seeing a therapist to help me come to terms with my trauma. My mom was and still continues to be one of my rocks.

My dad drove my mom and me to my post-op appointments in Philadelphia, Pennsylvania early in the mornings. He was always there to listen to me when I had told him about my retina appointments. Whenever I had a retinal detachment scare, and I would be shaking from the prospect of my retina detaching again, my dad would give me a hug, and he would reassure me that everything would be okay. I could no longer drive the go-carts, motor scooters, and dune buggies that became a big part of my identity. I felt terrible because I knew that he always loved sharing this interest with me. On the day that we gave away all of motor and electric vehicles that I had acquired over the years, I expressed to my dad how devastating I was that this period of my life was over. My dad looked at me, and he said, "That's okay, Steph, we had a lot of fun, but now we will find other hobbies to enjoy together. Your safety is all that matters to me."

Both of my parents took turns driving me to and from my university so that I could attend my classes. To be honest, those moments were some of the best moments of my life. My mom

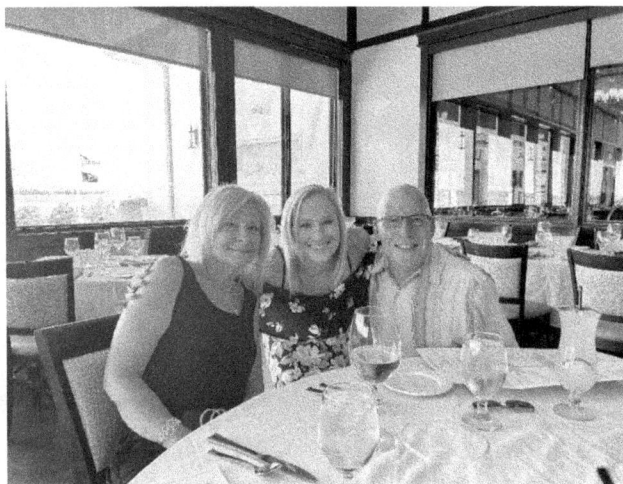

Figure 17. My mom, Diane (left), and my dad, Paul (right) on my 32nd birthday celebration

Photo by Stephanie Levin (2024d).

and I would stop at Dunkin' Donuts to get iced coffee, and as she drove me to school, we would talk and listen to the radio. My dad would pick me up from school at night, and we would stop at Taco Bell for a late dinner. I would talk to him and tell him about my classes and what I was currently learning. Although I could not drive at the time, I would not take back these moments because I was able to spend time with my parents that I would not have gotten to do so otherwise. To show you what my parents look like, Figure 17 is a picture of my parents and me that was taken in June 2024 (Levin, 2024).

My friends

I have four incredible friends who have stuck by me through thick and thin. Each of these women was instrumental in my recovery process and the years after my surgeries. My two best friends, Mary and Maizie, never once complained about having to pick me up or drive me to an event that we were going to. They were the first two friends that my mom called hysterically crying when we had received news about my retina detaching. Mary and Maizie also visited me while I was at home recovering from my surgeries. They never judged me or viewed me differently. To them, I was still the same Stephanie who they knew from second grade and from our freshman year of high school. They supported me when I graduated with my Master in Business Administration (MBA) degree (Levin, 2018), and they continue to be a source of strength and support as I pursue my doctorate degree in educational leadership (see Figure 18).

Figure 18. I (middle), Mary (left), and Maizie (right) at my MBA graduation Photo by Stephanie Levin (2018).

Figure 19. I (left) and Lori (right)

Photo by Stephanie Levin (2017).

I met my friend, Lori, while I was a sophomore in college (Levin, 2017). We were taking a class together called *Quantitative Business Methods,* and we instantly became fast friends. To this day, Lori was and is one of the most understanding individuals about my condition. She never questioned my limitations, and she always encouraged me to rest my eyes and not do anything overly strenuous. Whenever I told her about other people who reacted negatively to my limitations, she would always stand by my side. To this day, we are still good friends, and I cherish our friendship built over the years (see Figure 19).

Shefali was another friend of mine whom I had met in college (Levin, 2019) (see Figure 20). Shefali acted as a safe haven for

Figure 20. Shefali (left) and I (right)

Photo by Stephanie Levin (2019).

me. I would often talk to her about my experiences with hav-
ing undergone eye surgery and the subsequent vision loss that
I had endured after my second surgery. As I told her every single
detail, she would sit there and listen to me vent. At that time, all
I needed was someone to listen to me, and Shefali did just that.
She made me feel like I was being heard.

Sue: My vision technician

Sue was an integral person in my healing journey. I remember
the first day I met my vision technician who would have a lasting
impact on my life. In January 2015, a few weeks after my second

surgery, I was sitting in the waiting room with my mom. I was terrified of what my retina specialist was going to find during that day's examination. At that point, I began to realize that I had permanent vision loss in my right eye, and I was having a difficult time coming to terms with my new reality. In addition, I was scared that a new detachment would be discovered at this appointment, and I would need to be rushed back to Wills Eye Hospital for yet another surgery. As I sat in the waiting room with my mom, I heard a voice say, "Stephanie." I knew that it was my turn to be seen, and on shaky legs, I walked towards the person who would be my vision technician for the day. With kind eyes and a warm smile, my nurse introduced herself as Sue. As Sue led me back to the first examination room, my heart started to pound harder by the second. I sat down in the chair, and Sue proceeded to ask me if I was seeing any new flashes, floaters, or black curtains within my field of vision. These are the telltale signs that retinal detachment may be occurring, so it was important that I was honest with my vision tech. In response to Sue's questions, I croaked, "No."

As time went on, and I began to see Sue consistently for my retina examinations. My vision tech now began to ask me questions about my life. During one of my appointments, I had explained that I had needed to take a semester off from school to heal from my second retinal detachment, and I expressed my sadness and frustration over having to make this decision. I loved going to school, and I felt as though my life had been put on hold. Sue stopped what she was doing, looked at me, and said, "You have been through a lot. Right now, your sole concern should be getting better." Up until that point, I was not allowing myself to understand that what I was going through was life-changing, and I was not permitting myself to grieve my circumstances. At that moment, Sue gave me that permission that I was subconsciously denying myself. Back then, I was a perfectionist, and I was under so much pressure to bounce back from this situation. I wanted to be the poster child of resilience, and I wanted to show the world that this situation did not beat me. However, healing is neither instantaneous nor linear. Everyone's healing journey is different, and looking back, I should have given myself permission to realize that it is okay not to be okay.

Over the years, Sue has continued to be my source of strength at my retina appointments. Currently, I find myself not feeling as nervous as I once felt when I go to my annual retina checks. I will admit, subconsciously, I still feel apprehension when I go to my appointments, and by the end of the day, when I have received a clean bill of health, I find myself feeling mentally and physically drained from the day's events. Truthfully, I do not think that I will ever stop feeling this way. However, whenever I see Sue now, I express excitement when I tell her about my latest life updates. I tell Sue all about my doctoral career, my current job, and any other events that are happening in my life. Sue was and is a mother figure to me, and I cannot begin to thank her for always being a source of calm during a storm of uncertainty.

Time for therapy

In 2019, I began to see a therapist to help me come to terms with my experiences. I was 27 years old at the time, and my life path was in a downward spiral. It felt like I was stuck in neutral while my friends and acquaintances were moving forward in their lives. My mom was the one who felt that I needed to talk to someone. I remember fighting her tooth and nail on this idea. Back then, I did not want to admit that I had a problem. I felt like I would be further stigmatized by having to see a therapist. But my behavior was out of control. My relationships with my family were suffering deeply. I was acting out in ways that were uncharacteristic to me. For example, if my family attempted to talk to me, I would respond to their questions in a condescending way. I would scream at them to get my points across, and I did not know how to communicate my feelings in a healthy manner. In addition to the ongoing arguments with my family, my outlook on life became extremely pessimistic. With every passing day, I could not find one thing that I was grateful for. Also, my relationships outside of my family were toxic. In this world, you are supposed to surround yourself with people who will have a positive impact on your life. That was not the case for me. Instead of surrounding myself with positive people, I made the conscious decision to surround myself with negative people. These people ultimately brought me further down into the depths of despair, and I allowed them to have this impact on me.

The truth was, I had this idea that everyone was out to get me, and I portrayed myself as the victim. I was angry at my circumstances, and the pain that plagued me was relentless. As I envisioned my life, I found myself at a crossroads with no direction in mind. Up until this point, I always knew what my next steps were going to be. I was a planner, and I was proud of that fact. However, I will admit, I did not have any plans. I was going around and around in one big circle, and I needed professional help to pull me out of this unhealthy cycle that I had created for myself.

Breakthrough

I remember my first therapy session like it was yesterday. I walked into the room and sat down on the couch. I told my therapist all about my life, my retinal detachments, the passing of my grandmother and gramps, and other sources of trauma that had significantly impacted me. As I went into detail about my life, I remember breaking down into large, heaving sobs. I just sat on the couch, and I cried. I cried for everything that I had lost and for the person who I once was. I cried for the missed opportunities and for all of the horrible things that people had said to me while on my journey. I cried for the loss of my grandmother and gramps. I sobbed over the fact that my grandmother would never see me graduate from college when all I had wanted was for her to be there during that significant moment. I cried until I had no more tears left to cry.

I wish that I could tell you that all of my problems were solved that day during my first therapy session. Unfortunately, that could not be further from the truth. My healing journey was filled with peaks and valleys. It was not pretty by any stretch of imagination. There were days when I felt like I had figured everything out, and there were other days when I had failed miserably. With the help of therapy, it took a total of five years to accept what had happened to me and to realize that the old Stephanie would never be coming back. But I had to do the work to become better. I had regular therapy sessions with my therapist. While I was attending therapy, I began to document what I was feeling in a journal. I always enjoyed writing, so this exercise really helped me especially when I was having three therapy sessions a week. In addition to therapy and journaling, I visited my family physician, and under the direction of my doctor, I began taking medicine to treat my depression and anxiety.

As I look back at that period of my life, I am so happy that I had decided to take these steps to heal. Mental health and wellness are nothing to be ashamed of. We all struggle at some point, and it is by using these resources that we can give ourselves the opportunity to become whole again. If I had not decided to take control of my life, I cannot imagine where I would be today. I would probably still be going down that same dark path without a light to illuminate the way. I think it is important that we give ourselves grace during difficult times, and to accept when we are not okay. However, it is up to us to change the course of our lives and to begin to do the work that will ultimately set us free.

Who I am today

I am happy to tell you that I have accepted my newfound identity as a visually impaired woman. I no longer look back on my experiences with shame and disgust. Instead, I rejoice over the fact that not only did I survive this period of my life but also I thrived. I am proud of the resilience that I have demonstrated during my journey. After my surgeries, I had to relearn everything. I had to relearn how to drive, I had to relearn how to be human, and I had to learn how to love myself again. I am happy to tell you that because of my strong support system and my own determination, I was able to forge ahead. Today, I am able to drive a car. Although I have some trouble driving at night when in unfamiliar places, and my eyes tend to get tired towards the end of the day,

I have found that I can, for the most part, drive independently. I still find myself getting anxious when behind the wheel, but I have learned to calm myself down so that I can safely drive myself to my destination.

Through therapy, I have learned how to properly communicate my feelings. Some days, I make mistakes, and I find myself reverting to my old way of communicating with others. However, I tell myself that I am only human and tomorrow will be a better day. I still have feelings of anxiety that creep in from time to time, but I am aware of these emotions, and I ask myself why I am feeling this way. When I get to the root cause of these feelings, I take a deep breath and think, "It is okay to feel this way. Your feelings are valid, and they matter."

New opportunities

My experiences led me to a career as a doctoral candidate who focuses on ways in which higher education can provide equitable environments for students with disabilities. In addition, my journey has provided me with so many opportunities to help other individuals who are like me. For example, I have had the pleasure to speak openly about my experiences on a LinkedIn Live episode and on a lived experiences panel for the New Jersey Commission for the Blind and Visually Impaired. Recently, I became an advocacy subcommittee member for the New Jersey Association of Blind Students. I am also a member of the New Jersey Federation of the Blind. I have found that through my experiences, I am able to help change the way in which disability is viewed at the higher education and societal levels. My life has a purpose, and it has meaning.

Figure 21. I on my 32nd birthday celebration

Photo by Stephanie Levin (2024c).

Today, when I look at myself in the mirror, I see a strong woman smiling back at me. I marvel at how far this person has come, and how their journey is not yet finished (Levin, 2024). Staring at my reflection, I see beauty (see Figure 21).

Conclusion

Within Chapter 7, I took you on my journey towards reclaiming my self-identity as a visually impaired woman. The last and final chapter of this book, which is Chapter 8, will emphasize how advocacy and empathy are needed to address disability within higher education. In addition, I will discuss ways in which all-inclusiveness can be promoted for students with disabilities while on their college and university campuses.

8
Advocacy and empathy: We have to do better

We have reached the last chapter of this book! After reading through seven important chapters pertaining to disability, I think that we can all agree that we need to do better when it comes to addressing the needs of higher education students with disabilities. Let my story serve as an example that we need to start enacting some serious changes within the walls of our institutions. This ongoing cycle of disability stigma, discrimination, mental health challenges, and judgment cannot continue. As a disability advocate, this is a call to action to start changing our current disability rhetoric. The questions that beg to be answered are the following: What can we do to start enacting change? How can we do better? In this next section, I highlight some ways that we can implement inclusive practices within higher education that will promote equitable change.

Be an advocate

To truly take steps towards equitable change, you need to become an advocate for the disability community. To be a disability advocate is to guarantee that the rights and requests of individuals with disabilities are satisfied (NorthEast Independent Living Services, 2024). I recommend joining advocacy groups for individuals with disabilities. In terms of visual impairment, some of the advocacy groups that disability advocates can join include the American Foundation for the Blind, the National Federation of the Blind, the American Council of the Blind, and the New Jersey Association of Blind Students.

Be a source of comfort within the classroom

Faculty need to act as a source of comfort for students with disabilities. Ultimately, in order to be that source of comfort, educators need to undergo proper training. It is true that many times, faculty do not know how to manage students with disabilities within their classrooms. I recommend that disability curriculum and training programs be enacted for incoming and current educators. The good news is that there are some higher education institutions offering disability training for their faculty and staff. For example, Rutgers, which is the State University of New Jersey, provides accessibility training for faculty who are teaching students who have disabilities (Rutgers, The State University of New Jersey, 2024b). However, the questions that become apparent are how many faculty members are actually using this training? Are faculty even aware of these resources? This is where systems thinking needs to enter into the equation.

Use systems thinking

The truth is that providing information about students with disabilities on higher education websites on disability and accessibility is a small part of the puzzle. Ableism within higher education is a systemic problem. It is a problem that is rooted in discriminatory practices and social injustice. During my doctoral studies, I have had the pleasure of reading the book titled *Systems Thinking for Social Change* by David Peter Stroh. I highly recommend this book because it sets the foundation for enacting systemic change within your given context. In Stroh's (2015) book, there is an illustration in which five individuals are looking at an elephant. One individual equates an elephant to a tree trunk, while another individual equates an elephant to a brush (Stroh, 2015). Ultimately, each division and department within higher education believes that it is seeing the picture of disability in its entirety. However, that idea could not be further from the truth. College and university campuses need to effectively collaborate so that the needs of students with disabilities can be served (Lalor, Madaus, and Newman, 2020, cited in Levin, 2024). Real change starts with these collaborative efforts. All of this important work pertaining to disability cannot be put upon one division or department. A complex problem such as this requires thoughtful solutions that address the root causes.

How did we get to this point?

Before we address the institutional systems as a whole, I believe that the very first step in enacting change is to ask ourselves how we have gotten to this point. Why is it that we view students with disabilities differently than those students who do not have a disability? Where did we come up with this idea of normality? I am here to debunk the myth that has plagued our society for eons: No one person is normal. Everyone is different, and I believe that it is our differences that make us who we are. However, to dismantle these ideas of normalcy, we need to be aware of ourselves. How do we start this process of awareness? Well, the first step is to undergo thorough examinations of our beliefs and values pertaining to disability. In addition to conducting this analysis, we need to understand how our current identities as educators affect our relationships with students with disabilities. If we do not allow ourselves to explore our current identities, and we continue to be unaware of who we are as educators, then real, substantial change will not be implemented (Ortiz and Patton, 2012).

In addition to examining our identities, we need to understand disability from a historical context. Context allows us to comprehend the significance of a problem and its structure (Belanger, 2006, cited in Mueller and Broido, 2012). I think that there is a lack of awareness as to what this community has endured from a historical standpoint. I feel that it is important that we, as educators, learn about disability. Chapter 1 in this book highlights some of the key components within disability history and higher education; however, there are additional readings that can provide you with more insight into the history of disability. I will include this resource under the additional readings section of this book.

Start talking

We need to have difficult conversations regarding disability. I know, having these challenging conversations is no easy feat. Enacting change is risky business, and there is a significant chance that we may encounter resistance from others when trying to improve our institutional culture. However, it is by having those difficult conversations that we may begin to deconstruct our biases and assumptions pertaining to disability. Once these initial thought processes are dismantled, we can begin to reconstruct them into principles that are rooted in social justice (Dugan, 2017).

Disability promotion

Faculty need to promote disability services within their classrooms. Just including disability resources on syllabi or providing pamphlets that list these resources during class will make a difference. Educators can also discuss disability services with their students on the first day of class.

Incorporate disability within community, belonging, access, and engagement efforts

Recall that in Chapter 5, I discussed the lack of disability awareness within community, belonging, access, and engagement initiatives. Personally, I believe that disability needs to be incorporated more into community, belonging, access, and engagement efforts. How are we going to raise awareness pertaining to disability without it being promoted by community, belonging, access, and engagement? The answer is the following: We will not.

Be kind

Finally, the most important thing that we can do for students with disabilities is to be kind. As educators, we need to show our students that we care for them and their well-being. If, after your first day of class is dismissed, a student approaches you, and they explain to you that they have a disability, please show kindness towards them. It took so much courage from that student to approach you and explain their circumstances. Listen to what your student has to say. Look them in the eye and reassure them that you will advocate for them. We have a responsibility to ensure that students with disabilities have the right to be successful, and those chances for success start with us.

Conclusion

My friends, this is the end of my book and the end of my story. In Chapter 1, I provided you with a foundational understanding of disability history within higher education. We explored key events pertaining to disability such as the passage of Section 504 of the Rehabilitation Act of 1973, the Americans with Disabilities Act of 1990 and its amendment, and the Capitol Crawl of 1990, to name a few. We learned how intricate the history of disability within higher education actually is, and how students with disabilities were treated within this context. Chapter 2 explored the current disability landscape within higher education and while we have come a long way in our initiatives, statistical evidence has shown that students with disabilities still experience stigmatization and discrimination while attending their colleges and universities. In Chapter 3, we defined the term *visual impairment,* and we explored the causes of visual impairment such as retinal detachment, glaucoma, aniridia, and amblyopia. In addition, I shed some light on some of the symptoms that you can expect when experiencing a visual impairment such as blurred vision, sensitivity to light, and tunnel vision. By reading Chapters 4 and 5, we explored disability stigma, ableism, and the barriers that students with visual impairments face while attending their college or university of choice. Some of the barriers that students with visual impairments experience pertain to issues with accommodations, issues with admissions, and issues with access to technology.

Throughout this book, in addition to providing you with practical and theoretical knowledge pertaining to disability within higher education, I walked you through my own journey as a visually impaired woman. I shared with you some very personal experiences that up until this point were unknown to the majority of people. Chapter 6 focused specifically on the mental health struggles that I had encountered while healing from my surgeries. We discussed my struggles with PTSD, depression, and anxiety, and how higher education students as a whole are susceptible to either new traumatic events, or they carry a lifetime of trauma that bleeds into other facets of their lives. In Chapter 7, I discussed my healing journey, and how I came to terms with my newfound identity. I explained to you the steps that I took to become whole again, and I learned how to love the person who I had become. My journey was not an easy one; however, I had a strong support system that helped me to find my way. The final chapter, Chapter 8, addressed ways in which we as educators can provide inclusive environments for higher education students with disabilities. Some of these methods include being an advocate, acting as a source of comfort within a classroom setting, community, belonging, access, and engagement, and practicing kindness towards students with disabilities.

The purpose of this book was twofold: In these chapters, I set out to educate you about disability within higher education and tell you my story of becoming visually impaired while attending college. My biggest hope is that my story raises awareness regarding the many challenges that higher education students with visual impairments experience. Additionally, I want nothing more than to see equitable change enacted for the entire disability community. I hope that this book serves as one of the many catalysts for this necessary change to take place. Once upon a time, I was made to feel ashamed of my disability. Today, that cycle of shame has come to an end. I no longer carry the pain that once inflicted me. The pain is now replaced with acceptance, compassion, and understanding for my experiences. My disability is a part of who I am, and, like a badge of honor, I wear this identity proudly.

Before this book ends, I would like to once more introduce myself. My name is Stephanie Levin, and I am a visually impaired woman. I am alive now more than ever, and I am beautiful just the way that I am. At this point, I want to thank you for reading this book and for allowing me to pick up the pieces with you.

Suggested discussion questions and assignments

1. **Discussion question:** As stated in Chapter 1, the history of disability within higher education is quite intricate. Ultimately, this community fought relentlessly to be seen, and to be heard. For this discussion question, I invite you to go beyond the context of disability within higher education. Please research the 504 Sit-In that took place in 1977. In addition, look up an activist who was instrumental in having Section 504 of the Rehabilitation Act of 1973 regulated. Please provide the following points within your response:

    A. What was the purpose of the 504 Sit-In?
    B. What is the name of your chosen activist?
    C. What did your chosen activist do that helped to regulate Section 504?
    D. What was the result of the 504 Sit-In?

2. **Discussion question:** Research your college or university's accommodation policy for students with disabilities. In two to three paragraphs, please include the following points within your response:

    A. How easy or difficult was it to find your college or university's accommodation policy?

B. What federal laws for disability are cited within your institution's accommodation policy?

C. What changes would you make to the existing policy?

D. What aspects of the policy would you keep the same?

3. **Discussion question:** In Chapter 3, we defined the term *visual impairment,* and I provided you with a brief description of some of the causes of visual impairment such as amblyopia, aniridia, retinal detachment, etc. In one to two paragraphs, identify one cause of visual impairment that was not discussed within this course book. Please include the following information within your responses:

A. The name of your visual impairment condition.

B. A brief description of the condition.

C. How this condition affects an individual's everyday life.

D. How this condition is treated (if applicable).

E. One photo to illustrate your condition.

4. **Assignment:** Recall in Chapter 5 that only the medical and social models of disability were identified and discussed. For this assignment, pick one model of disability that was not discussed within this course book. In one to two pages, please provide the following information:

A. Identify your chosen model of disability.

B. Describe in detail the premise of your chosen model.

C. If applicable, discuss the origins of your model of disability. For example, who was the person who established your chosen model?

D. Do you agree or disagree with the premise of your chosen disability model? Why or why not?

5.   **Assignment:** In Chapters 5 and 8 of this course book, I
     have discussed that there is a lack of awareness and initia-
     tives pertaining to disability within community, belonging,
     access, and engagement efforts at higher education insti-
     tutions. In groups of two or three, please review a college or
     university's student success, engagement, belonging, and
     access website. The institution that you choose to review
     may be either public or private. Please create a 5- to 10-slide
     presentation which addresses the following components:

     A.   The name of the institution.
     B.   The name of the institution's student success, engage-
          ment, belonging, and access division.
     C.   The director of the institution's student success,
          engagement, belonging, and access division.
     D.   Upon reviewing your chosen institution's student
          success, engagement, belonging, and access website,
          what resources to raise awareness for disability are
          available for faculty, staff, and students?
     E.   If your institution of choice provides student success,
          engagement, belonging, and access resources for dis-
          ability, what additional resources would you add to
          this list?
     F.   If your institution of choice does not provide stu-
          dent success, engagement, belonging, and access
          resources for disability, what are some of the resources
          that you would provide?

References

abbé R. A. L. (1742–1842). *Sicard*. [Online]. Available at: commons. wikimedia.org [Accessed 27 June 2024].

ADA National Network. (2015). *A planning guide for making temporary events accessible to people with disabilities*. [Online]. Available at: adata.org/guide/planning-guide-making-temporary-events-accessible-people-disabilities [Accessed 1 June 2024].

ADA National Network. (2024). *What are a public or private college-university's responsibilities to students with disabilities?* [Online]. Available at: adata.org [Accessed 1 June 2024].

Adams K. S. and Proctor B. E. (2010). Adaption to College for Students with and without Disabilities: Group Differences and Predictors. *Journal of Postsecondary Education and Disability*, 22(3), pp.166–184. Available at: https://files.eric.ed.gov/fulltext/EJ906691.pdf [Accessed 14 December 2024].

Adreon, D. and Durocher, J. S. (2007). Evaluating the College Transition Needs of Individuals with High-Functioning Autism Spectrum Disorders. *Intervention in School and Clinic*, 42(5), pp. 271–279. Available at: https://journals-sagepub-com.ezproxy.rowan.edu/doi/epdf/10.1177/10534512070420050201 [Accessed 14 December 2024].

AHEAD. (2024). *Overview*. [Online]. Available at: www.ahead.org/about-ahead/about-overview [Accessed 16 June 2024].

Albee, G. W. (1977). Problems in Living Are Not Sicknesses: Psychotherapy Should Not Be Covered under National Health Insurance. *The Clinical Psychologist*, 30(3). Available at: https://psycnet.apa.org/record/1979-34489-001 [Accessed 25 August 2024].

Al-Jarf, R. (2021). Periscope as a Tool for Delivering Live Academic Lectures. *Journal of Educational Technology,* 18(1), pp. 15–25. Available at: www.proquest.com/docview/2577748907?accoun tid=13605&parentSessionId=sxj56KvER7K4y0r8obki1tB5lQ9 0mX%2BT1A3RXJeO8jI%3D&pq- origsite=primo&sourcetype= Scholarly%20Journals [Accessed 14 December 2024].

American College Health Association. (2022). *American-College Health Association-National College Health Assessment III: Undergraduate Student Reference Group Data Report Spring 2022.* [PDF] Silver Spring, MD: American College Health Association. Available at: www.acha.org/wp-content/uploads/ 2024/07/NCHA-III_SPRING_2022_UNDERGRAD_REFERENCE_GR OUP_DATA_REPORT.pdf [Accessed 14 December 2024].

American College Health Association. (2023). *American-College Health Association-National College Health Assessment III: Undergraduate Student Reference Group Data Report Spring 2023.* [PDF] Silver Spring, MD: American College Health Association. Available at: www.acha.org/wp-content/uploads/ 2024/07/NCHA-III_SPRING_2023_UNDERGRAD_REFERENCE_GR OUP_DATA_REPORT.pdf [Accessed 14 December 2024].

American Optometric Association. (n.d.). *Hyperopia (farsightedness).* [Online]. Available at: www.aoa.org/healthy-eyes/eye-and-vision-conditions/hyperopia?sso=y [Accessed 7 July 2024].

American Society of Retina Specialists. (2024a). *Glossary.* [Online]. Available at: www.asrs.org/patients/retinal-diseases/10/gloss ary#Retinal-detachment [Accessed 18 May 2024].

American Society of Retina Specialists. (2024b). *Lattice degeneration.* [Online]. Available at: www.asrs.org/patients/reti nal-diseases/36/lattice-degeneration [Accessed 18 May 2024].

Americans with Disabilities Act of 1990 (1990), Pub. L. No. 101–336, 104 Stat. 328.

Aquino, K. C. and Bittinger, J. D. (2019) The Self-(un)Identification of Disability in Higher Education. *Journal of Postsecondary Education and Disability,* 32(1), pp. 5–19. Available at: https://web-p-ebscohost-com.ezproxy.rowan.edu/ehost/pdfviewer/pdfviewer?vid=0&sid=859f328a-f8be-43b2-a6e8-ac023c51c530%40redis [Accessed 14 December 2024].

Asch, A. (1998). Distracted by Disability. *Cambridge Quarterly of Healthcare Ethics*, 7(1), pp. 77–87. Available at: www-cambridge-org.ezproxy.rowan.edu/core/journals/cambridge-quarterly-of-healthcare-ethics/article/distracted-by-disability/0D4509AEFB1B473DBC4B720EB8E66D08 [Accessed 14 December 2024].

Barker, R. G., Wright, B. A., and Gonick, M. R. (1946). *Adjustment to Physical Handicap and Illness: A Survey of the Social Psychology of Physique and Disability.* Brooklyn, NY: Social Science Research Council.

Barker, R. G. (1948). The Social Psychology of Physical Disability. *Journal of Social Issues,* 4. Available at: The Social Psychology of Physical Disability - Barker - 1948 - Journal of Social Issues - Wiley Online Library [Accessed 25 August 2024].

Barnes, C. (1990). *Cabbage Syndrome: The Social Construction of Dependence.* London, UK: Falmer Press.

Barry, A. E., Whiteman, S. D., and Wadsworth, S. M. (2014). Student Service Members/Veterans in Higher Education: A Systematic Review. *Journal of Student Affairs Research and Practice*, 51(1). Available at: www-tandfonline-com.ezproxy.rowan.edu/doi/pdf/10.1515/jsarp-2014-0003?needAccess=true [Accessed 26 May 2024].

Barton, L. (2018). Sociology and disability: Some emerging issues. In: L. Barton, ed., *Disability and Society: Emerging Issues and Insights.* London: Routledge, pp. 3–17.

Baynton, D. C. (2013). Disability and the justification of inequality in American history. In: L. J. Davis, ed., *The Disability Studies Reader.* London: Routledge, pp. 17–33.

Begelman, D. A. (1971). Misnaming, Metaphors, the Medical Model, and Some Muddles. *Psychiatry*, 34(1), pp. 38–58. Available at: www.tandfonline.com/doi/abs/10.1080/00332 747.1971.11023655 [Accessed 25 August 2024].

Beilke, J. R. and Yssel, N. (1999). The Chilly Climate for Students with Disabilities in Higher Education. *College Student Journal*, 33(3), pp. 364–364. Available at: https://go-gale-com.ezproxy. rowan.edu/ps/i.do?p=AONE&u=rowan&id=GALE%7CA62839 444&v=2.1&it=r&aty=ip [Accessed 20 June 2024].

Belanger, C. (2006). What is the meaning of "historical context"? . In: *Quebec History Encyclopedia*. Available at: faculty.marianopolis. edu/c.belanger/quebechistory/Historicalcontext.html [Accessed 2 November 2024]

Beratan, G. D. (2006). Institutionalizing Inequity: Ableism, Racism and IDEA 2004, *Disability Studies Quarterly*, 26(2). Available at: https://dsq-sds.org/index.php/dsq/article/view/682 [Accessed 27 July 2024].

Besser Eye Care Team. (2023). *International day of persons with disabilities: Visual impairment*. [Blog] Eduardo Besser MD. Available at: www.eduardobessermd.com/blog/visual-impairm ent-characteristics#:~:text=There%20are%20a%20number%20 of,patient%20has%20a%20visual%20impairment. [Accessed 6 July 2024].

Binder, K. W., Wrzesińska, M. A., and Kocur, J. (2020). Anxiety in Persons with Visual Impairment. *Psychiatr Pol*, 54(2), pp. 279–288. Available at: https://pubmed.ncbi.nlm.nih.gov/32772060/2 [Accessed 2 November 2024].

Bingham, C., Clarke, L., Michielsens, E., and Van De Meer, M. (2013). Towards a Social Model Approach? British and Dutch Disability Policies in the Health Sector Compared. *Personnel Review*, 42(5), pp. 613–637. Available at: www.emerald.com/insi ght/content/doi/10.1108/PR-08-2011-0120/full/html [Accessed 25 August 2024].

Blasey, J., Wang, C., and Blasey, R. (2023). Accommodation Use and Academic Outcomes for College Students with Disabilities. *Psychological Reports*, 126(4), pp. 1891–1909. Available at: https://journals-sagepub-com.ezproxy.rowan.edu/doi/epub/10.1177/00332941221078011 [Accessed 7 June 2024].

Bogart, K, Logan, S. W., Hospodar, C., Woekel, E, and Corrigan, P. W. (2019). Disability Models and Attitudes among College Students with and without Disabilities. *Stigma and Health (Washington, D.C.)*, 4(3), pp. 260–263. Available at: www.proquest.com/docview/2041431640?accountid=13605&parentSessionId=fUYHso0Y8YuOt7t40lpQ4SWFDptPr9wFFkiWM2RFblU%3D&pq-origsite=primo&sourcetype=Scholarly%20Journals [Accessed 24 July 2024].

Bonsaksen, T. et al. (2022). Post-Traumatic Stress Disorder in People with Visual Impairment Compared with the General Population. *International Journal of Environmental Research and Public Health*, 19(2), pp. 619–619. Available at: www.proquest.com/docview/2621294524?accountid=13605&parentSessionId=hk63vQpWKyolHAuvxUeK8N14VG67172v5FHnhui6qiw%3D&pq-origsite=primo&sourcetype=Scholarly%20Journals [Accessed 2 November 2024].

Boyd, K., McKinney, J. K., and Turbert, D. (2023). What is glaucoma? Symptoms, causes, diagnosis, treatment. [Online]. American Academy of Ophthalmology. Available at: www.aao.org/eye-health/diseases/what-is-glaucoma [Accessed 7 July 2024].

BrainyQuote. (2024). *John Clifford quotes*. [Online] Available at: www.brainyquote.com/quotes/john_clifford_397572 [Accessed 18 June 2024].

Brown, S. E. (2002). What Is Disability Culture? *Disability Studies Quarterly*, 22(2). Available at: https://dsq-sds.org/index.php/dsq/article/view/343/433#:~:text=Instead%20disability%20culture%20is%20a,but%20what%20we%20have%20created. [Accessed 25 August 2024].

Brown, S. E. (2003). *Movie Stars and Sensuous Scars: Essays on the Journey from Disability Shame to Disability Pride.* Bloomington, IN: IUniverse.

Brown, S. E. (2008). Breaking barriers: The pioneering disability students services program at the University of Illinois, 1948–1960. In: E. H. Tamura, ed., *The History of Discrimination in U.S. Education: Marginality, Agency, and Power.* New York, NY: Palgrave Macmillan, pp. 165–192.

Bryant, J. and Welding, L. (2024). College Student Mental Health Statistics. *Best Colleges.* [Online] 1–22. Available at: www.bestcolleges.com/research/college-student-mental-health-statistics/

Burch, S. and Longmore, P. K. (2009). Disability Rights Movement. In: *American Disability History.*1. New York, NY: Facts on File. (pp. 280–285). Available at: https://handicapcenter.com/wp-content/uploads/2014/05/Encyclopedia-of-American-Disability-History.pdf [Accessed 14 December 2024].

Cahoon, J. and Pettey, J. (2016). *Congenital Aniridia.* [Online]. Available at: morancore.utah.edu/section-12-retina-and-vitreous/aniridia/ [Accessed 2 November 2024].

Carnival of Souls. (1962). [Movie] Lawrence, Kansas: Harcourt Productions.

Center for Accessible Living. (n.d.). *The advocado press at the center for accessible living.* [Online] Available at: www.calky.org/advocado-press [Accessed 25 August 2024].

Centre for Equitable Library Access. (2024). *What is a print disability?* [Online] Available at: celalibrary.ca/about-us/what-is-a-print-disability [Accessed 16 June 2024].

CDC. (2024a). *About vision loss and mental health.* [Online] Available at: www.cdc.gov/vision-health/about-eye-disorders/vision-loss-mental-health.html#:~:text=Vision%20loss%20has%20been%20linked,loss%20reported%20anxiety%20or%20depression. [Accessed 2 November 2024].

CDC. (2024b). *Common barriers to participation experienced by people with disabilities.* [Online] Available at: www.cdc.gov/disability-inclusion/barriers/?CDC_AAref_Val=www.cdc.gov/ncbddd/disabilityandhealth/disability-barriers.html [Accessed 5 January 2025].

CDC. (2024c). *Prevalence estimates for vision loss and blindness.* [Online] Available at: www.cdc.gov/vision-health-data/prevalence-estimates/vision-loss-prevalence.html [Accessed 21 August 2024].

Chamberlain, C. (2024). Tim Nugent: The father of accessibility. *United States Olympic & Paralympic Museum ™,* [Online] 1–7. Available at: usopm.org/tim-nugent-the-father-of-accessibility/ [Accessed 27 May 2024].

Chamusco, B. G. (2017). Revitalizing the Law That "Preceded the Movement": Associational Discrimination and the Rehabilitation Act of 1973. *The University of Chicago Law Review.* 84(3), pp. 1285–1324. Available at: www.jstor.org/stable/26457107 [Accessed 1 June 2024].

Chatterjee, L. and Mitra, M. (1998). Evolution of Federal and State Policies for Persons with Disability in the United States: Efficiency and Welfare Impacts. *The Annals of Regional Science,* 32(3), pp. 347–365. Available at: https://web-p-ebscohost-com.ezproxy.rowan.edu/ehost/pdfviewer/pdfviewer?vid=0&sid=f09e96ab-88ac-40f7-980a-06d2693ed348%40redis [Accessed 26 May 2024].

Cleveland Clinic. (2022a). *Blindness.* [Online] Available at: my.clevelandclinic.org/health/diseases/24446-blindness [Accessed 7 July 2024].

Cleveland Clinic. (2022b). *Macula.* [Online] Available at: my.clevelandclinic.org/health/body/23185-macula [Accessed 25 May 24].

Cleveland Clinic. (2024). *Albinism.* [Online] Available at: my.clevelandclinic.org/health/diseases/21747-albinism [Accessed 3 July 2024].

Cooke, K. (2021). *Amblyopia.* [Online]. Available at: mansfieldvi-sion.net/tx/amblyopia-lazy-eye/ [Accessed 28 August 2024].

Cornell University. (2024). *Universal design for learning.* [Online] Available at: teaching.cornell.edu/teaching-resources/designing-your-course/universal-design-learning [Accessed 25 August 2024].

D'Andrea, F. M. (2012). Preferences and Practices among Students Who Read Braille and Use Assistive Technology. *Journal of Visual Impairment & Blindness,* 106(10), pp. 585–596.

Davidson, S. (n.d.). *Trauma-Informed Practices for Postsecondary Education: A Guide.* 1. [PDF] Portland, OR: Education Northwest, pp. 1–28. Available at: https://educationnorthwest.org/sites/defa ult/files/resources/trauma-informed-practices-postsecondary-508.pdf [Accessed 2 November 2024].

Davis, L. J. (2006). Constructing normalcy: The bell curve, the novel, and the invention of the disabled body in the nineteenth century. In: L. J. Davis, ed., *The Disability Studies Reader.* 2nd ed. New York, NY: Rutledge, pp. 3–16.

de Lorenzo, D. (2009). Gallaudet University. In: S. Burch ed., *Encyclopedia of American Disability History* (vol. 2). New York, NY: Facts on File, pp. 394– 396.

Dictionary.com. (2024). Barrier. In: *Random House Unabridged Dictionary*, Broadway, New York City: Penguin Random House, LLC, p. 1. Available at: www.dictionary.com/browse/barrier [Accessed 24 August 2024].

Disability Rights North Carolina. (2021). *ADA title ii (State and local government).* [Online] Available at: disabilityrightsnc.org

Disabled American Veterans. (2024). *About DAV.* [Online] Available at: www.dav.org/about-dav/ [Accessed 26 May 2024].

Dowd, M. (1996). The 1980s: June 25, 1989; The Education of Dan Quayle. *The New York Times Magazine*, [Online] 1–3. Available at: www.nytimes.com/1996/04/14/magazine/the-1980-s-june-25-1989-the-education-of-dan-quayle.html [Accessed 19 June 2024].

Drake, R. F. (2018). A critique of the role of the traditional charities. In: L. Barton, ed., *Disability and Society: Emerging Issues and Insights*. London: Routledge, pp. 147–166.

Dugan, J. P. (2017). *Leadership Theory: Cultivating Critical Perspectives*. San Francisco, CA: Jossey-Bass.

Dunn, D. S. (2011). Situations Matter: Teaching the Lewinian Link between Social Psychology and Rehabilitation Psychology. *Journal of the History of Psychology*, 14(4). Available at: www.proquest.com/docview/886596480?accountid=13605&parentSessionId=X7yR%2F4BfcpCWgAfsFFdHqRXpc3ylk2Hdcw0xj1UpCTo%3D&pq-origsite=primo&sourcetype=Scholarly%20Journals [Accessed 25 August 2024].

Ervin, M. (2009). *The founder of the Disability Rag tells its story*. [Blog] Media dis&dat. Available at: media-dis-n-dat.blogspot.com/2009/04/founder-of-disability-rag-tells-its.html [Accessed 25 August 2024].

Evans, N. J. (2008). Theoretical foundations of universal instructional design. In: J. L. Higbee and E. Goff, eds., *Pedagogy and Student Services for Institutional Transformation: Implementing Universal Design in Higher Education*. Minneapolis, MN: University of Minnesota, Center for Research on Developmental Education and Urban Literary, College of Education and Human Development, pp. 11–23.

Evans, J., Broido, E. M., Brown, K. R., Wilke, A. K., and Herriott, T. K. (2017). *Disability in Higher Education: A Social Justice Approach*. 1. [eBook] San Francisco, California: Jossey-Bass. Available at: https://ebookcentral.proquest.com/lib/rowan/reader.action?docID=4816152&ppg=3 [Accessed 26 May 2024].

Felitti, V. J. et al. (1998). Relationship of Childhood Abuse and Household Dysfunction to Many of the Leading Causes of Death in Adults: The Adverse Childhood Experiences (ACE) Study.

American Journal of Preventive Medicine, 14(4), pp. 245–258. Available at: www.ajpmonline.org/article/S0749-3797(98)00017-8/pdf [Accessed 2 November 2024].

Fenderson, D. A. (1984). Opportunities for Psychologists in Disability Research. *American Psychologist,* 39(5), pp. 524–528. Available at: www.proquest.com/docview/614299364?accoun tid=13605&parentSessionId=HEuJED7NB5%2BmP%2BooXZ up7qqAeaxRaaMC5s94C09Bg%2BQ%3D&pq-origsite=primo&-sourcetype=Scholarly%20Journals [Accessed 25 August 2024].

Fierros, E. G. (2006). One Size Does Not Fit All: A Response to Institutionalizing Inequity. *Disability Studies Quarterly*, 26(2). Available at: https://dsq-sds.org/index.php/dsq/article/view/683 [Accessed 27 July 2024].

Fitzgerald, H. (2006). Disability and physical education. In: D. Kirk, D. MacDonald, and M. O'Sullivan, eds., *The Handbook of Physical Education*. London: SAGE, pp. 752–766.

Flintoff, A., Fitzgerald, H., and Scraton, S. (2008). The Challenges of Intersectionality: Researching Difference in Physical Education. *International Studies in Sociology of Education*, 18(2), pp. 73–85. Available at: www-tandfonline-com.ezproxy.rowan.edu/doi/pdf/10.1080/09620210802351300?needAccess=true [Accessed 25 August 2024].

Forsbach T. A. and Rice-Mason J. (2001). College Students' Utilization and Perceptions of Disability Support Services. *Academic Exchange Quarterly,* 5(2), p. 113.

Friedman, C. and Owen, A. L. (2017). Defining Disability: Understandings of and Attitudes towards Ableism and Disability. *Disability Studies Quarterly,* 37(1). Available at: https://dsq-sds.org/index.php/dsq/article/view/5061 [Accessed 25 August 2024].

Galatzer-Levy, I. R. et al. (2012). Coping Flexibility, Potentially Traumatic Life Events, and Resilience: A Prospective Study of College Student Adjustment. *Journal of Social and Clinical*

Psychology, 31(6), pp. 542–567. Available at: www.proquest.com/docview/1018687532?accountid=13605&parentSessionId=jUi7%2BskmQIThtOHX8FwonnNuWR6OIBfjvvQTgQRUo0w%3D&pq-origsite=primo&sourcetype=Scholarly%20Journals [Accessed 2 November 2024].

Gallaudet, E. M. (1888). *Life of Thomas Hopkins Gallaudet, Founder of Deaf-Mute Instruction in America*. 1. [PDF] New York, NY: H. Holt And Company 1888. Available at: archive.org/details/lifeofthomashopk00galluoft/page/n7/mode/2up?view=theater [Accessed 25 May 2024].

Gallaudet, E. M. 1983. *History of the College for the Deaf, 1857–1907*. Washington, DC: Gallaudet College Press.

Gelber, S. (2005). A 'Hard-Boiled Order': The Reeducation of Disabled WWI Veterans in New York City. *Journal of Social History*, 39(1), pp. 161–180. Available at: https://muse-jhu-edu.ezproxy.rowan.edu/article/187567 [Accessed 26 May 2024].

Getzel, E. E. (2008). Addressing the Persistence and Retention of Students with Disabilities in Higher Education: Incorporating Key Strategies and Supports on Campus. *Exceptionality: The Official Journal of the Division for Research of the Council for Exceptional Children*, 16(4), pp. 207–219. Available at: www-tandfonline-com.ezproxy.rowan.edu/doi/full/10.1080/09362830802412216 [Accessed 25 August 2024].

Gifford, E. E. (2021). Gallaudet's Vision Advances Deaf Education. [Online] Available at: connecticuthistory.org/gallaudets-vision-advances-deaf-education/ [Accessed 25 May 2024].

Gill, C. J., Kewman, D. G., and Brannon, R. W. (2003). Transforming Psychological Practice and Society: Policies That Reflect the New Paradigm. *American Psychologist*, 58(4), pp. 305–312. Available at: www.proquest.com/docview/614448990?accountid=13605&parentSessionId=I8RbAn2PvNyVNOSwEF8GN6YVjs%2FMSQV5CfLB6zhkdnw%3D&pq-origsite=primo&sourcetype=Scholarly%20Journals [Accessed 25 August 2024].

Goffman, E. (1961). *Asylums: Essays on the Social Situation of Mental Patients and Other Inmates.* Garden City, NY: Doubleday & Company.

Goffman, E. (1963). *Stigma: Notes on the Management of Spoiled Identity.* Englewood Cliffs, NJ: Prentice-Hall.

Goodley, D., Lawthom, R., and Liddiard, K. (2021). Key Concerns for Critical Disability Studies. *International Journal of Disability and Social Justice,* 1(1), pp. 27–49. Available at: www-jstor-org.ezproxy. rowan.edu/stable/10.13169/intljofdissocjus.1.1.0027 [Accessed 25 August 2024].

Griffin, P., Peters, M. L., and Smith, R. M. (2007). Ableism curricular design. In: M. Adams, L. A. Bell and P. Griffin, eds., *Teaching for Diversity and Social Justice.* 2nd ed. New York, NY: Routledge, pp. 335–358.

Haegele, J. A. and Hodge, S. (2016). Disability Discourse: Overview and Critiques of the Medical and Social Models. *Quest (National Association for Kinesiology in Higher Education),* 68(2), pp. 193–206. Available at: https://web-p-ebscohost-com.ezproxy.rowan.edu/ plink?key=100.65.114.34_8000_1936156967&site= ehost&scope=site&db=s3h&AN=114515294&crl=f&appTo ken=e105304f-f1af-4fd6-a371-7a38f9ec96b0 [Accessed 25 August 2024].

HealthLink BC. (n.d.). *Scleral buckle surgery for retinal detachment.* [Online] Available at: www.healthlinkbc.ca/health-topics/scleral-buckling-surgery-retinal-detachment#:~:text=Scleral%20buckling%20surgery%20is%20a,the%20white%20of%20the%20eye) [Accessed 18 May 2024].

Healthy Aging RRTC. (n.d.). *Disability stigma and your patients.* [Online] Available at: agerrtc.washington.edu/info/factsheets/ stigma#:~:text=Concealment%20–%20If%20possible%2C%20 some%20people,also%20forgo%20some%20medical%20ser-vices. [Accessed 24 July 2024].

Hickel, K. W. (2001). Medicine, bureaucracy, and social welfare: The politics of disability compensation for American veterans of World War I. In P. K. Longmore and L. Umansky eds., *The New Disability History: American Perspectives*. New York: New York University Press, pp. 236–267.

Hoch, A., Stewart, D., Webb, K., and Wyandt-Hiebert, M. A. (2015). Trauma-Informed Care on a College Campus. In: *The Annual Meeting of the American College Health Association*. [Online] Orlando: The American College Health Association, pp. 1–105.

Hogan, A. J. (2019). Social and Medical Models of Disability and Mental Health: Evolution and Renewal. *CMAJ: Canadian Medical Association Journal=Journal de L'Association Medicale Canadienne*, 191(1), pp. E16–E18. Available at: www.cmaj.ca/content/191/1/E16 [Accessed 25 August 2024].

Holt, M., Gillen, D., Nandlall, S. D., Setter, K., Thorman, P., Kane, S. A., Miller, C. H., Cook, C., and Supalo, C. (2019). Making Physics Courses Accessible for Blind Students: Strategies for Course Administration, Class Meetings, and Course Materials. *The Physics Teacher*. 57(2), pp. 94–98. Available at: https://pubs-aip-org.ezproxy.rowan.edu/aapt/pte/article/57/2/94/362043/Making-Physics-Courses-Accessible-for-Blind [Accessed 1 June 2024].

Imrie, R. (1997). Rethinking the Relationships between Disability, Rehabilitation, and Society. *Disability and Rehabilitation*, 19(7), pp. 263–271. Available at: www-tandfonline-com.ezproxy.rowan.edu/doi/pdf/10.3109/09638289709166537?needAccess=true [Accessed 20 June 2024].

Invitation to Dance. (2014). Directed by Gene Kelly [Motion Picture] United States: Metuffer Films.

Johns Hopkins Medicine. (2024). *What is vitrectomy?* [Online] Available at: www.hopkinsmedicine.org/health/wellness-and-prevention/vitrectomy [Accessed 18 May 2024].

Kamaghe, J., Luhanga, E., and Kisangiri, M. (2020). The Challenges of Adopting M-learning Assistive Technologies for Visually Impaired

Learners in Higher Learning Institution in Tanzania. *International Journal of Emerging Technologies in Learning*, 15(1), pp. 140–151. Available at: www.proquest.com/docview/2666940348?accoun tid=13605&parentSessionId=ZGm8JMcjIc3LiULVgpprf7X4 1QO%2FZgwvreBl%2F15JtKk%3D&pq-origsite=primo&sourcet ype=Scholarly%20Journals [Accessed 25 August 2024].

Kapperman, G., Kelly, S. M., and Koster, E. (2018). Using the JAWS Screen Reader and the Focus Braille Display to Read Foreign Language Books Downloaded from the Bookshare Accessible Online Library. *Journal of Visual Impairment & Blindness*, 112(4), pp. 415–419. Available at: https://go-gale-com.ezproxy.rowan. edu/ps/i.do?p=AONE&u=rowan&id=GALE%7CA669352759&v= 2.1&it=r [Accessed 25 August 2024].

Kattari, S. K. (2017). Development of the Ableist Microaggression Scale and Assessing the Relationship of Ableist Microaggressions with the Mental Health of Disabled Adults. *Journal of Social Service Research*, 45(3), pp. 400–417. Available at: www-tandfonline-com.ezproxy.rowan.edu/doi/pdf/10.1080/01488376.2018.1480 565?needAccess=true [Accessed 14 December 2024].

Keenan, W. R. et al. (2019). Impact of the Americans with Disabilities Act Amendments Act on Documentation for Students with Disabilities in Transition to College: Implications for Practitioners. *Career Development and Transition for Exceptional Individuals*, 42(1), pp. 56–63. Available at: https://journals.sagepub.com/doi/pdf/10.1177/2165143418809691 [Accessed 16 June 2024].

Kenneth Spencer Research Library Archive Collections. (n.d.). *John Clifford papers*. [Online]. Available at: archives.lib.ku.edu/repositories/3/resources/3341 [Accessed 18 June 2024].

Kija, L. L. and Mgumba, B. F. (2024). Reducing Barriers for Inclusion of Students with Visual Impairments in the Universities: Focus on Educational and Psychological Needs. *The British Journal of Visual Impairment*. Available at: https://journals-sagepub-com.ezproxy. rowan.edu/doi/epub/10.1177/02646196231225061 [Accessed 25 August 2024].

Kilpatrick, D. G. et al. (2003). Violence and Risk of PTSD, Major Depression, Substance Abuse/Dependence, and Comorbidity: Results from the National Survey of Adolescents. *Journal of Consulting and Clinical Psychology*, 71(4), pp. 692–700. Available at: www.proquest.com/docview/614385880?accoun tid=13605&parentSessionId=eJAImyF0%2BkSbh8poFW%2B-NHG800IU3Zm%2BeZV0nN0Tsj84%3D&pq-origsite=primo&sou rcetype=Scholarly%20Journals [Accessed 2 November 2024].

Kim, S. Y. (2021). College Disability Support Offices as Advertisements: A Multimodal Discourse Analysis. *Discourse Studies*, 23(2), pp. 166–190. Available at: https://journals-sage pub-com.ezproxy.rowan.edu/doi/epub/10.1177/146144562 0966921 [Accessed 16 June 2024].

Kisanga, D. H., and Kisanga, S. E. (2020). Access to Assistive Technology among Students with Visual Impairment in Higher Education Institutions in Tanzania: Challenges and Coping Mechanism. *University of Dar ess Salaam Library Journal*, 15(2). Available at: www.ajol.info/index.php/udslj/article/view/210786 [Accessed 25 August 2024].

Kitch, E. (1952). *AP Photo*. [Online]. Available at: www.wbur.org/ hereandnow/2015/11/12/tim-nugent-obituary [Accessed 27 May 2024].

Koch, L. C., Lo, W-J., Mamiseishvili, K., Lee, D., and Hill, J. (2018). The Effect of Learning Disabilities, Attention Deficit Hyperactivity Disorder, and Psychiatric Disabilities on Three-Year Persistence Outcomes at Four-Year Higher Education Institutions. *Journal of Vocational Rehabilitation*, 48(3), pp. 359–367, Available at: https:// web-p-ebscohost-com.ezproxy.rowan.edu/ehost/pdfviewer/ pdfviewer?vid=0&sid=91f0dfd1-fcad-4b8a-9210-3ea373dc5 d93%40redis [Accessed 14 December 2024].

Kudlick, C. J. (2001). The outlook of the problem and the prob-lem with the outlook: Two advocacy journals reinvent blind people in turn-of-the-century America. In: P. K. Longmore and

L. Umansky eds., *The New Disability History: American Perspectives*. New York: New York University Press, pp. 187–213.

Lalor, A. R., Madaus, J. W., and Newman, L. S. (2020). Leveraging Campus Collaboration to Better Serve All Students with Disabilities (Practice brief). *Journal of Postsecondary Education and Disability*, 33(3), pp. 249-255. Available at: https://web-p-ebscohost-com. ezproxy.rowan.edu/ehost/pdfviewer/pdfviewer?vid=0&sid= 5bac8360-3b8a-469b-8e90-631eabd480fb%40redis   [Accessed 17 June 2024].

Landsman, G. (2005). Mothers and Models of Disability. *The Journal of Medical Humanities*. [Online] 26(2–3), pp. 121–139. Available at: https://link-springer-com.ezproxy.rowan.edu/content/pdf/ 10.1007/s10912-005-2914-2.pdf [Accessed 14 December 2024].

Landsman, G. (2009). *Reconstructing Motherhood and Disability in the Age of "Perfect" Babies*. New York, NY: Routledge.

Lehrer-Stein, J. and Berger, J. (2023). A Path towards True Inclusion: Disabled Students and Higher Education in America. *International Journal of Discrimination and the Law*, 23(1–2), Available   at: https://journals-sagepbcom.ezproxy.rowan.edu/ doi/epub/10.1177/13582291231162215 [Accessed 17 June 2024].

Lemert, E. M. (1951). *Social Pathology: A Systematic Approach to the Theory of Sociopathic Behavior*. New York, NY: McGraw-Hill.

Lett, K., Tamaian, A., and Klest, B. (2020). Impact of Ableist Microaggressions on University Students with Self-Identified Disabilities. *Disability & Society*, 35(9), pp. 1441–1456. Available at: www-tandfonline-com.ezproxy.rowan.edu/doi/full/10.1080/ 09687599.2019.1680344 [Accessed 27 July 2024].

Levin, S. A. N. (2015). *Me wearing my sunglasses in June 2015, six months after my second retinal detachment surgery* [Photograph].

Levin, S. A. N. (2017). *Me (left) and Lori (right)*. [Photograph].

Levin, S. A. N. (2018). *Me (middle), Mary (left), and Maizie (right) at my MBA graduation.* [Photograph].

Levin, S. A. N. (2019). *Shefali (left) and me (right).* [Photograph].

Levin, S. A. N. (2024a). *Disabilities reported by higher education students bar chart* [Image].

Levin, S. A. N. (2024b). *Many students don't inform their colleges about their disability. That needs to change.* [Online] EdSurge. Available at: www.edsurge.com/news/2024-03-01-many-stude nts-don-t-inform-their-colleges-about-their-disability-that-needs-to-change [Accessed 17 June 2024].

Levin, S. A. N. (2024c). *Me on my 32nd birthday celebration* [Photograph].

Levin, S. A. N. (2024d). *My mom, Diane (left) and my dad, Paul (right) on my 32nd birthday celebration* [Photograph].

Levin, S. A. N. (2024e). *My right-eye vision* [Image].

Library of Congress. (1909). *Col. Charles R. Forbes, Director, US Veterans' Bureau.* [Online]. Available at: www.loc.gov/item/90/07 420 [Accessed 26 May 2024].

Longmore, P. K. (2003). *Why I Burned My Book and Other Essays on Disability.* Philadelphia, PA: Temple University Press.

Lourens, H. and Swartz, L. (2016). Experiences of Visually Impaired Students in Higher Education: Bodily Perspectives on Inclusive Education. *Disability & Society,* 31(2), pp. 240–251. Available at: www-tandfonline-com.ezproxy.rowan.edu/doi/full/10.1080/ 09687599.2016.1158092 [Accessed 25 August 2024].

Lukash, Z. (2021). *Human eye with clouded lens, white pupil, cataract macro stock photo.* [Online]. Available at: www.istockphoto.com/ photo/human-eye-with-clouded-lens-white-pupil-cataract-macro-gm1356560292-430698767 [Accessed 2 November 2024].

Ma, G. Y. K. and Mak, W. W. S. (2024). Maintenance of Ableist Society for Wheelchair Users: Roles of Medical Model of Disability and Witnessed Negotiation for Accessibility. *Disability & Society,* 39(9), pp. 2400–2425. Available at: www-tandfonline-com.ezproxy. rowan.edu/doi/full/10.1080/09687599.2023.2209277 [Accessed 25 August 2024].

Mackelprang, R. W. and Salsgiver, R. O. (2009). *Disability: A Diversity Model Approach in Human Service Practice.* Chicago, IL: Lyceum Books.

Madaus, J. W. (2000). Services for College and University Students with Disabilities: A Historical Perspective. *Journal of Postsecondary Education and Disability,* 14(1), pp. 4–21.

Madaus, J. W. and Shaw, S. F. (2004). Section 504: Differences in the Regulations for Secondary and Postsecondary Education. *Intervention in School and Clinic,* 40(2), pp. 81–87. Available at: https://doi-org.ezproxy.rowan.edu/10.1177/1053451204040 0020301 [Accessed 1 June 2024].

Madaus, J. W. (2011). The History of Disability Services in Higher Education. *New Directions for Higher Education*, 2011(154), pp. 5–15. Available at: https://onlinelibrary-wiley-com.ezproxy.rowan. edu/doi/epdf/10.1002/he.429 [Accessed 25 May 2024].

Madaus, J. W., Kowitt, J. S., and Lalor, A. (2012). The Higher Education Opportunity Act: Impact on Students with Disabilities. *Rehabilitation Research, Policy, and Education,* 26(1), pp. 33–42.

Manago, B., Davis, J. L., and Goar, C. (2017). Discourse in Action: Parents' Use of Medical and Social Models to Resist Disability Stigma. *Social Science & Medicine (1982),* pp.169–177. Available at: www-sciencedirect-com.ezproxy.rowan.edu/scie nce/article/pii/S027795361730309X [Accessed 1 June 2024].

Mayo Clinic Staff. (2021). *Lazy eye (amblyopia).* [Online] Available at: www.mayoclinic.org/diseases-conditions/lazy-eye/symptoms-causes/syc-20352391 [Accessed 2 September 2024].

Mayo Clinic Staff. (2022a). *Cataracts*. [Online] Available at: www.mayoclinic.org/diseases-conditions/depression/symptoms-causes/syc-20356007 [Accessed 2 November 2024].

Mayo Clinic Staff. (2022b). *Depression (major depressive disorder)*. [Online] Available at: www.mayoclinic.org/diseases-conditions/cataracts/symptoms-causes/syc-20353790 [Accessed 6 July 2024].

McEnaney, L. (2011). Veterans' Welfare, the GI Bill and American Demobilization. *The Journal of Law, Medicine & Ethics*, 39(1), pp. 41–47. Available at: https://doi.org/10.1111/j.1748-720X.2011.00547.x [Accessed 26 May 2024].

McLean, D. (1971). *American pie*. [Medium]. Cold Spring, NY: United Artists. Available at: www.songfacts.com/lyrics/don-mclean/american-pie [Accessed 18 May 2024].

Miller, L. A., Lewandowski, L. J., and Antshel, K. M. (2015). Effects of Extended Time for College Students with and without ADHD. *Journal of Attention Disorders*, 19(8), pp. 678–686. Available at: https://journals-sagepub-com.ezproxy.rowan.edu/doi/epub/10.1177/1087054713483308 [Accessed 17 June 2024].

Mueller, J. A. and Broido, E. M. (2012). Historical context: Who we were is part of who we are. In: J. Arminio, V. Torres, and R. L. Pope, eds., *Why Aren't We There Yet? Taking Personal Responsibility for Creating an Inclusive Campus*. Sterling, VA: Stylus, pp. 57–101.

Murphy, K. L. (2021). Civil Rights Laws: Americans with Disabilities Act of 1990 and Section 504 of the Rehabilitation Act of 1973: I.A. v. Seguin Indep. Sch. Dist. 881 F. Supp. 2d 770. *Journal of Physical Education, Recreation & Dance*, 92(1), pp. 57–59. Available at: www-tandfonline-com.ezproxy.rowan.edu/doi/pdf/10.1080/07303084.2021.1844555?needAccess=true [Accessed 1 June 2024].

National Center for Education Statistics. (n.d.). *Students with dsabilities*. [Online]. Available at: nces.ed.gov/fastfacts/display.asp?id=60 [Accessed 14 June 2024].

National Council on Disability. (2013). *About us.* [Online] Available at: www.ncd.gov/about-us/

National Eye Institute. (2024a). *Color blindness.* [Online] Available at: www.nei.nih.gov/learn-about-eye-health/eye-conditions-and-diseases/color-blindness#:~:text=What%20is%20color%20blindn ess%3F,vision%20deficiency%20runs%20in%20families. [Accessed 7 July 2024].

National Eye Institute. (2024b). *Retinal detachment.* [Online] Available at: www.nei.nih.gov/learn-about-eye-health/eye-conditions-and-diseases/retinal-detachment [Accessed 2 November 2024].

National Institute of Mental Health. (2024). *What is post-traumatic stress disorder (PTSD)?* [Online] Available at: www.nimh.nih.gov/ health/topics/post-traumatic-stress-disorder-ptsd [Accessed 2 November 2024].

National Institute of Neurological Disorders and Stroke. (2023). *Learning disabilities.* [Online] Available at: www.ninds.nih.gov/ health-information/disorders/learning-disabilities#:~:text= Learning%20disabilities%20are%20disorders%20that,Coordin ate%20movements [Accessed 16 June 2024].

National Museum of Health and Medicine. (1919). *Disabled WWI veteran at Walter Reed General Hospital.* [Online] Available at: www. kpbs.org/news/arts-culture/2015/11/09/debt-honor-disabled-veterans-american-history [Accessed 27 June 2024].

Newman L., Wagner M., Knokey A. M., Marder C., Nagle K., Shaver D., and Schwarting M. (2011). *The Post-High School Outcomes of Young Adults with Disabilities Up to 8 Years After High School. A Report from the National Longitudinal Transition Study-2 (NLTS2) (NCSER 2011–3005).* 1. Washington, D.C.: U.S. Department of Education. Available at: https://ies.ed.gov/ncser/pubs/20113 005/pdf/20113005.pdf [Accessed 14 December 2024].

Nielsen, K. (2012). *A Disability History of the United States.* Boston, MA: Beacon Press.

NorthEast Independent Living Services. (2024). *The importance of disability advocacy*. [Online] Available at: www.neils.org/the-imp ortance-of-disability-advocacy/ [Accessed 2 November 2024].

O'Donnell, M. L. et al. (2004). Posttraumatic Stress Disorder and Depression Following Trauma: Understanding Comorbidity. *The American Journal of Psychiatry*, 161(8), pp. 1390–1396. Available at: https://psychiatryonline-org.ezproxy.rowan.edu/doi/10.1176/ appi.ajp.161.8.1390 [Accessed 2 November 2024].

Olkin, R., Pledger, C, and Norman, A. B. (2003). Can Disability Studies and Psychology Join Hands? *American Psychologist,* 58(4), pp. 296–304. Available at: www.proquest.com/docview/614377 709?accountid=13605&parentSessionId=cXfazwCGdRTRnWbo0 gifDt3C%2F3MWsBvLKF7X8jCwnn0%3D&pq-origsite=primo&- sourcetype=Scholarly%20Journals [Accessed 25 August 2024].

Olkin, R. (2022). *Conceptualizing disability: Three models of disability*. [Online] American Psychological Association. Available at: www.apa.org/ed/precollege/psychology-teacher- network/introductory-psychology/disability-models [Accessed 25 August 2024].

Oliver, M. (1983). *Social Work with Disabled People*. London, UK: Red Globe Press.

Oliver M. (1990). *The Politics of Disablement*. London, UK: Macmillan.

Oliver, M. (2004). The social model in action: If I had a hammer. In: C. Barnes and G. Mercer, eds., *Implementing the Social Model of Disability: Theory and Research*. Leeds: The Disability Press, pp. 18–31.

Opie, J. (2018). Technology Today: Inclusive or Exclusionary for Students with Vision Impairment? *International Journal of Disability, Development and Education,* 65(6), pp. 649–663. Available at: https://web-p-ebscohost-com.ezproxy.rowan.edu/ ehost/pdfviewer/pdfviewer?vid=0&sid=3d4fbe65-f032-4196- ba64-656929995ac4%40redis [Accessed 25 August 2024].

Ortiz, A. M. and Patton, L. D. (2012). Awareness of self. In: J. Arminio, V. Torres, and R.L. Pope, eds., *Why Aren't We There Yet? Taking Personal Responsibility for Creating an Inclusive Campus*. Sterling, Va: Stylus, pp. 9–31.

Oslund, C. (2015). *Disability Services and Disability Studies in Higher Education: History, Contexts, and Social Impacts*. 1. [eBook] New York, NY: Palgrave Macmillan US. Available at: https://ebook central.proquest.com/lib/rowan/detail.action?pq-origsite= primo&docID=1873962 [Accessed 2 June 2024].

Ostrowski, C. P. (2016). Improving Access to Accommodations: Reducing Political and Institutional Barriers for Canadian Postsecondary Students with Visual Impairments. *Journal of Visual Impairment & Blindness*, 110(1), pp. 15–25. Available at: https://go-gale-com.ezproxy.rowan.edu/ps/i.do?p= AONE&u=rowan&id=GALE%7CA444403307&v=2.1&it=r&aty=ip [Accessed 25 August 2024].

Palmer, M. and Harley, D. (2012). Models and Measurement in Disability: An International Review. *Health Policy and Planning*, 27(5), pp. 357–364. Available at: https://academic.oup.com/hea pol/article/27/5/357/749458 [Accessed 25 August 2024].

Parsons, T. (1951). *The Social System*. Glencoe, IL: Free Press.

Partow, S., Cook, R., and McDonald, R. (2021). Coping with Stigmatization and Discrimination Related to Blindness and Low Vision. *Rehabilitation Psychology*, 66(4), pp. 576–588. Available at: www. proquest.com/docview/2564572165?parentSessionId=iOkp1lE3A DYeBehQZyzt%2BcxRlCjNGoIY%2BiU3bf1tdMw%3D&pq-origs ite=primo&accountid=13605&sourcetype=Scholarly%20Journals [Accessed 24 July 2024].

Pavithran, S. D. (2017). *Expert consensus on barriers to college and university online education for students with blindness and low vision*. Doctor of Philosophy. Utah State University.

Pelka, F. (2012). *What We Have Done: An Oral History of the Disability Rights Movement*. Amherst, MA: University of Massachusetts Press.

Perkins School for the Blind. (2023). *5 myths about print disabilities.* [Online] Available at: www.perkins.org/resource/5-myths-about-print-disabilities/ [Accessed 16 June 2024].

Perkins School for the Blind. (2024). *What is ableism?* [Online] Available at: www.perkins.org/what-is-ableism/ [Accessed 27 July 2024].

Peters, S. J. (2024). Disability culture. In: *The Editors of Encyclopaedia Brittanica* (eds.). Chicago, IL: Brittanica. Available at: www.britann ica.com/topic/ableism [Accessed 25 August 2024].

Peterson, D. B. and Aguiar, L. (2004). History and systems: United States. In: T. F. Rigger and D. R. Maki, eds., *Handbook of Rehabilitation Counseling.* New York: Springer Publishing Company, pp. 50–75.

Porter, D. and Gregori, N. Z. (2023). *What is lattice degeneration?* [Online] Available at: www.aao.org/eye-health/diseases/what-is-lattice-degeneration [Accessed 18 May 2024].

Reed, M. and Curtis, K. (2012). Experiences of Students with Visual Impairments in Canadian Higher Education. *Journal of Visual Impairment & Blindness,* 106. Available at: Experiences of students with visual impairments in Canadian higher education. (apa.org) [Accessed 25 August 2024].

Riddell, S. (2018). Theorizing special education needs in a changing political climate. In: L. Barton, ed., *Disability and Society: Emerging Issues and Insights.* London: Routledge, pp. 83–106.

Rosa, N. M. et al. (2016). Teaching about Disability in Psychology: An Analysis of Disability Curricula in U.S. Undergraduate Psychology Programs. *Teaching of Psychology,* 43(1), pp. 59–62. Available at: https://journals-sagepub-com.ezproxy.rowan.edu/doi/full/ 10.1177/0098628315620885 [Accessed 25 August 2024].

Rothman, B. (1988). *The song that never ends.* [Online] New York City: A&M Records. Available at: The Kiboomers - This Is the Song That Never Ends Lyrics | Lyrics.com [Accessed 14 December 2024].

Rowan University Office of Accessibility Services. (2024). *Acquiring accommodations*. [Online] Available at: sites.rowan.edu/accessibilityservices/firstyearstudents.html [Accessed 17 June 2024].

Rozalski, M. et al. (2010). Americans with Disabilities Act Amendments of 2008. *Journal of Disability Policy Studies*, 21(1), pp. 22–28. Available at: https://libkey.io/libraries/600/articles/5550009/full-text-file [Accessed 2 June 2024].

Rutgers-New Brunswick Office of Disability Services. (2024a). *Common accommodations*. [Online] Available at: ods.rutgers.edu/students/common-accommodations [Accessed 17 June 2024].

Rutgers, The State University of New Jersey. (2024b). *Faculty training on accessibility*. Available at: radr.rutgers.edu/resource/faculty-training-accessibility [Accessed 2 November 2024].

Rytwinski, N. K. et al. (2013). The Co-Occurrence of Major Depressive Disorder among Individuals with Posttraumatic Stress Disorder: A Meta-Analysis. *Journal of Traumatic Stress*, 26(3), pp. 299–309. Available at: https://web-p-ebscohost-com.ezproxy.rowan.edu/ehost/pdfviewer/pdfviewer?vid=0&sid=0addd5d5-8277-41a0-a38e-dddc7711afe4%40redis [Accessed 2 November 2024].

Salvin, J. (2016). *Visual impairment*. [Online] Nemours Teens Health. Available at: www.kidshealth.org/en/teens/visual-impairment.html [Accessed 6 July 2024].

Scheef, A., Caniglia, C., and Barrio, B. L. (2020). Disability as Diversity: Perspectives of Institutions of Higher Education in the U.S. *Journal of Postsecondary Education and Disability*, 33(1), pp. 49–61. Available at: https://web-p-ebscohost-com.ezproxy.rowan.edu/ehost/pdfviewer/pdfviewer?vid=0&sid=166907ea-6f58-4cbe-9e46-bdb1329fcfb4%40redis [Accessed 14 December 2024].

Scott, S. S., McGuire, J. M., and Shaw, S. F. (2003). Universal Design for Instruction: A New Paradigm for Adult Instruction in

Postsecondary Education. *Remedial and Special Education*, 24(6), pp. 369–379. Available at: www.proquest.com/docview/57122 334?accountid=13605&parentSessionId=AOlkG2Mn4S2d1zRt9S 0yetHGUyssRWLnBLmU08WGA%2Bk%3D&pq-origsite=primo&-sourcetype=Scholarly%20Journals [Accessed 25 August 2024].

Section 504 of the Rehabilitation Act of 1973, 29 U.S.C. § 794 (1973).

Shakespeare, T. (2013). *Disability Rights and Wrongs Revisited.* London, UK: Routledge.

Shallish, L. (2015). "Just How Much Diversity Will the Law Permit?": The Americans with Disabilities Act, Diversity and Disability in Higher Education. *Disability Studies Quarterly*, 35(3). Available at: https://dsq-sds.org/index.php/dsq/article/view/4942 [Accessed 18 May 2024].

Singh v. George Washington University School of Medicine and Health Sciences [2007] 508 F.3d 1097.

Skudra, N. (2023). *Jennifer Keelan-Chaffins: An iconic child activist.* [Online] Available at: www.di-nc.org [Accessed 2 June 2024].

Smith, I. and Mueller, C. O. (2022). The Importance of Disability Identity, Self-Advocacy, and Disability Activism. *Inclusive Practices*, 1(2), pp. 47–54. Available at: https://journals-sagepub-com.ezproxy.rowan.edu/doi/epub/10.1177/27324745211057155 [Accessed 27 May 2024].

Smith, P. (2004). Whiteness, Normal Theory, and Disability Studies, *Disability Studies Quarterly*, 24(2). [Online] Available at: https://dsq-sds.org/index.php/dsq/article/view/491 [Accessed 14 December 2024].

Snyder, T. D., de Brey, C. and Dillow, S. A. (2016). Digest of Education Statistics 2015. Available at: https://nces.ed.gov/pubsearch/pubsinfo.asp?pubid=2016014 [Accessed 14 December 2024].

Soria, K. S. (2021). *Supporting Undergraduate Students with Disabilities: A Focus on Campus Climate and Sense of Belonging.*

1. [PDF] Washington, D.C.: U.S. Department of Education. Available at: https://ici-s.umn.edu/files/dFiDERA9Dh/supporting_undergraduate_students_with_disabilities [Accessed 14 December 2024].

Sparabary, A., Kelley, S., and Romack, J. (2021). *Guide for visually impaired college students*. All About Vision. [Online] Available at: www.allaboutvision.com/resources/guide-for-visually-impaired-college-students/ [Accessed 25 August 2024].

Spears, V. (2019). *AHEAD*. [Online]. Available at: www.ahead.org/events-programming/conferences/2019-equity-and-excellence/2019-pricing [Accessed 26 June 2024].

Stevens, R. (2017). *A Time of Scandal: Charles R. Forbes, Warren G. Harding, and the Making of the Veterans Bureau*. 1.[ebook] Baltimore: Johns Hopkins University Press. Available at: https://doi.org/10.1353/book.72129 [Accessed 26 May 2024].

Stroh, D. P. (2015). *Systems Thinking for Social Change: A Practical Guide to Solving Complex Problems, Avoiding Unintended Consequences, and Achieving Lasting Results*. White River Junction, VT: Chelsea Green Publishing.

Strom, R. J. (1950). *The Disabled College Veteran of World War II*. Washington, DC: American Council on Education.

Sutherland, A. (1989). Disability arts, disability politics. In: *Movin' On, A Festival of Arts by Disabled People*. [Online] London, pp. 1–5.

Szasz, T. S. (1956). Some Observations on the Relationship between Psychiatry and the Law. *A.M.A. Archives of Neurology and Psychiatry*, 75(3), pp. 297–315. Available at: https://jamanetwork.com/journals/archneurpsyc/article-abstract/652168 [Accessed 25 August 2024].

Szasz, T. S. (1960). The Myth of Mental Illness. *American Psychologist*, 15(2), pp. 113–118. Available at: https://psycnet.apa.org/doiLanding?doi=10.1037%2Fh0046535 [Accessed 25 August 2024].

The Advocado Press. (1983). *"The Disability Rag"*. [Online Image] Available at: harvester.lib.uidaho.edu/collection/items/lumber1716.html [Accessed 25 August 2024].

Thelin, J. R. (2004). *A History of American Higher Education*. Baltimore, MD: John Hopkins University Press.

Thelin, J. R. (2019). *A History of American Higher Education*. 3rd ed. Baltimore, MD: Johns Hopkins University Press.

Title II Subpart A of the Americans with Disabilities Act of 1990, 42 U.S.C. § 12132 (1990).

Tripathy, K. and Salini, B. (2023). Aniridia. In: *StatPearls [Internet]*. Treasure Island, FL: StatPearls Publishing, pp. 1–9. Available at: www.ncbi.nlm.nih.gov/books/NBK538133/ [Accessed 2 September 2024]

Tusler, A. (1977). *1977 San Francisco 504 Demonstration*. [Online] Available at: aboutdisability.com/index.php/nggallery/album/history?page_id=2764 [Accessed 1 June 2024].

UMass. (2024). *Understanding disability identity, community, and culture*. [Online] Available at: www.umassp.edu/inclusive-by-design/who-before-how/understanding-disabilities [Accessed 25 August 2024].

University of Illinois Archives. (1957). *Student in Wheelchair Rides Blue Bull Bus*. [Photograph]. Found in RS 16/6/11, Box 4, Folder Transportation 1957.

University of Illinois Archives. (2017). *Nugent, Timothy J. (1923-)*. [Online] Available at: https://archon.library.illinois.edu/archives/index.php?p=creators/creator&id=2347 [Accessed 27 May 2024].

UPIAS. (1976). *Fundamental Principles of Disability. Union of the Physically Impaired Against Segregation*.1. [PDF] Ealing, London: The Disability Alliance. Available at: disabledpeoplesarchive.com/wp-content/uploads/sites/39/2021//01/001-FundamentalPrinciplesOfDisability-UPIAS-DA-22Nov1975.pdf [Accessed 25 Aug. 2024]

U.S. Department of Education. (2016). *Digest of education statistics, 2015*. 51st Edition. [PDF] Washington: NCES, pp. 1–1042. Available at: https://nces.ed.gov/pubs2016/2016014.pdf [Accessed 25 August 2025].

U.S. Department of Education. (2017). *Characteristics and Outcomes of Undergraduates with Disabilities.* Available at: nces.ed.gov/pubs2018/2018432.pdf [Accessed 7 June 2024].

U.S. Department of Education. (n.d.). *Disability discrimination.* [Online] Available at: www2.ed.gov/about/offices/list/ocr/frontp age/faq/disability.html#dishar1 [Accessed 2 August 2024].

U.S. Department of Education. (2023). *Higher Education Opportunity Act-2008.* [Online] Available at: www2.ed.gov/pol icy/highered/leg/hea08/index.html [Accessed 16 June 21, 2024].

U.S. Department of Labor. (2009). *ADA Amendments Act of 2008 frequently asked questions.* [Online] Available at: www.dol.gov/ agencies/ofccp/faqs/americans-with-disabilities-act-amendme nts [Accessed 2 June 2024].

VectorMine. (2018). *Vector Illustration of Glaucoma Illness. Cross Section Comparison with Normal and Damaged Eye. Scheme with Cornea, Trabecular Meshwork and Aqueous Humor Fluid. Stock Illustration.* [Online]. Available at: www.istockphoto.com/vector/ vector-illustration-of-glaucoma-illness-cross-section-comparem ent-with-normal-and-gm998992914-270196240 [Accessed 2 November 2024].

Ward, M. J. (2009). A personal perspective on historical views of disability. In: C. E. Drum, G. L. Krahn, and H. Bersani eds., *Disability and Public Health*. Washington, DC: American Public Health Association, pp. 45–64.

Weinstein, R. M. (1994). Goffman's Asylums and the Total Institution Model of Mental Hospitals. *Psychiatry*, 57(4), pp. 348–367. Available at: www.tandfonline.com/doi/abs/10.1080/00332 747.1994.11024699 [Accessed 25 August 2024].

Weis, R. and Bittner, S. A. (2022). College Students' Access to Academic Accommodations over Time: Evidence of a Matthew Effect in Higher Education. *Psychological Injury and Law*, 15(3), pp. 236–252. Available at: https://link-springer-com.ezproxy.rowan. edu/content/pdf/10.1007/s12207-021-09429-7.pdf   [Accessed 17 June 2024].

Welding, L. (2023). Students with Disabilities in Higher Education: Facts and Statistics. *Best Colleges*. [Online] 1–16. Available at:.bestcolleges.com/research/students-with-disabilities-higher-education-statistics/#fn-15 [Accessed 14 December 2024].

Wendell, S. (1989). Toward a Feminist Theory of Disability. *Hypatia*, 4(2). Available at: https://www-jstor-org.ezproxy.rowan.edu/sta ble/pdf/3809809 {Accessed 31 January 2025].

Williams, G. (2001). Theorizing disability. An institutional history of disability. In: G. L. Albrecht, K. D. Seelman, and M. Bury, eds., *Handbook of Disability Studies*. Thousand Oaks: Sage Publications, pp. 123–144.

Wise, M. (2021). Oh What a Tangled Web We Weave When First We Practice To Deceive. *European Psychiatry*, 64(S1), pp. S24–S24. Available at: www.cambridge.org/core/services/aop-cambri dge-core/content/view/0F828E161BE3F7D380C95F5364868 1BB/S0924933821000894a.pdf/div-class-title-oh-what-a-tang led-web-we-weave-when-first-we-practice-to-deceive-div.pdf [Accessed 24 May 2024].

Wong v. Regents of the University of California [2005] 410 F.3d 1052.

World Health Organization. (2001). *International classification of functioning, disability and health (ICF)*. [Online] Available at: www. who.int/standards/classifications/international-classification-of-functioning-disability-and- [Accessed 24 August 2024].

World Health Organization. (2023a). *Anxiety disorders*. [Online] Available at: www.who.int/news-room/fact-sheets/detail/anxi ety-disorders [Accessed 2 November 2024].

World Health Organization. (2023b). *Blindness and vision impairment.* [Online] Available at: www.who.int/news-room/fact-sheets/detail/blindness-and-visual-impairment [Accessed 6 July 2024].

Wright, B. A. (1960). Physical Disability: A Psychosocial Approach. New York, NY: Harper Collins.

Wright, B. A. (1983). Physical Disability: A Psychosocial Approach. 2nd ed. New York, NY: Harper Collins.

Wright, G. F. (1851). *Posthumous oil painting of Thomas Hopkins Gallaudet.* [Online]. Available at: commons.wikimedia.org [Accessed 27 June 2024].

Wu, Y. (2018). *Perspectives of Graduate Students with Visual Impairments on Their Learning Experience in Online Education.* Doctor of Philosophy. George Mason University.

Zaks, Z. (2024). Changing the Medical Model of Disability to the Normalization Model of Disability: Clarifying the Past to Create a New Future Direction. *Disability and Society,* 39(12), pp. 3233–3260. Available at: www.tandfonline.com/doi/pdf/10.1080/09687599.2023.2255926?needAccess=true [Accessed 25 August 2024].

Zheutlin, J. D., Garber, F. W., and Glazer, L. C. (n.d.). *Activities after Vitrectomy or Scleral Buckle Surgery.* 1. [PDF] Grand Rapids, MI: Vitreo-Retinal Associates, P.C., 1–4). Available at: www.vrapc.com/wp-content/uploads/postop_vitrectomy_sb_20150130.pdf [Accessed 2 November 2024].

Zinn Education Project. (2024a). *April 28, 1977: Disability rights sit-ins force enactments of section 504.* [Online]. Available at: www.zinnedproject.org/news/tdih/sit-ins-force-504#:~:text=Between%20April%205%20and%20April,of%201973%20and%20publish%20regulations [Accessed 2 August 2024].

Zinn Education Project. (2024b). *March 12, 1990: Disability rights activists' "capitol crawl" for the ADA.* [Online]. Available at: www. zinnedproject.org/news/tdih/capitol-crawl-for-ADA/ [Accessed 1 June 2024].

Zhou, Z. (2023). Disabilities in Higher Education: Beyond "Accommodation". *Journal of Disability Studies in Education*, 3(2) pp.191–216. Available at: https://brill.com/view/journals/jdse/3/ 2/article-p191_004.xml [Accessed 24 July 2024].

For further reading and viewing

1. **Book:** *Disability in Higher Education: A Social Justice Approach (1st edition)* by Nancy J. Evans, Ellen M. Broido, Kirsten R. Brown, and Autumn K. Wilke. Available at: www.amazon.com/Disability-Higher-Education-Justice-Approach/dp/1118018222

2. **Documentary:** *Crip Camp: A Disability Revolution* by Nicole Newnham and James LeBrecht. Available on Netflix.

3. **Article:** *"Everyone is Normal, and Everyone has a Disability": Narratives of University Students with Visual Impairment* by: Nitsan Almog. Available at: www.cogitatiopress.com/socialinclusion/article/view/1697/942

4. **Article:** *When What Is Unseen Does Not Exist: Disclosure, Barriers and Supports for Students with Invisible Disabilities in Higher Education* by Anabel Moriña. Available at: www.tandfonline.com/doi/full/10.1080/09687599.2022.2113038

5. **Article:** *Making the Invisible Visible: Let's Discuss Invisible Disabilities* by Michael Edward Goodwin, BSc. Available at: https://eric.ed.gov/?id=EJ1294871

Additional resources

Advocacy groups

- **National Federation of the Blind:** https://nfb.org/
- **Commission for the Blind and Visually Impaired:** www.nj.gov/humanservices/cbvi/home/index.html
- **National Association of Blind Students:** https://nabslink.org/

Suicide and domestic violence resources

- **Suicide and Crisis Lifeline:** Dial 988
- **National Domestic Violence Hotline:** Call 1(800)-799-7233 or visit www.thehotline.org/

Support group

- **Retinal Detachment and/or Vitrectomy Support Group:** www.facebook.com/groups/683163888410622/

Index